Inside Secrets

CLUBHOUSE APP

WHAT EVERY ENTREPRENEUR NEEDS TO KNOW...

THE COMPREHENSIVE GUIDE

MULTIPLY YOUR IMPACT, MAXIMIZE YOUR INCOME, TARGET YOUR AUDIENCE & BUILD YOUR BRAND

ANDY BROADAWAY

Inside Secrets

CLUBHOUSE

What Every Entrepreneur Needs to Know...The Comprehensive Guide to: Multiply Your Impact, Maximize Your Income, Target your audience & Build Your Brand

Abundant Press - Las Vegas, NV 89107

www.AbundantPress.com

Ordering Information & Quantity Sales: Special discounts are available on quantity purchases by corporations, associations, and others. For details, contact the publisher. Orders by U.S. & International trade bookstores and wholesalers at: info@abundantpress.com. Printed in the United States of America- Library of Congress-in-Publication Data. Please note: This book was put together very quickly for a conference, so if you find errors, like spelling or grammar, please send us an email. Thank you.

Title: Inside Secrets Clubhouse APP

Sub-title: What Every Entrepreneur Needs to Know...The Comprehensive Guide to: Multiply Your Impact, Maximize Your Income, Target your audience & Build Your Brand

Author: Andy Broadaway

ISBN: 978-1-948287-25-8

1. The main category of the book — Business, Social Media, Marketing

First Edition, First Printing 1-15-2021

"Over the Shoulder"

STEP-BY-STEP

Training Videos

To get access visit:

ClubhouseTraining.APP

Inside Secrets

CLUBHOUSE

What Every Entrepreneur Needs to Know...The Comprehensive Guide to: Multiply Your Impact, Maximize Your Income, Target your audience & Build Your Brand

Table of Contents

Chapter One:
Introduction - Answering the Invitation

The internet world is buzzing about a relatively new application in the social media genre. Not another one, you think. Aren't there enough of these kinds of sites already? Why do we need another one?

Let me tell you that this one is different. Clubhouse App is an *audio,* social media application. That's right. There is no texting, no typing, no emojis. Clubhouse is an application where you actually "listen" to what others have to say, and you get to "talk" as well. This app is not only different; at the moment, it is unique.

Maybe it is in response to the pandemic and the "Zoom" explosion. Without regular face to face contact, many of us are hungry to hear each other's voices. Yet, we are not able to "Zoom" with a hundred people. However, on Clubhouse, you can have a conversation that might involve tens of people or even a hundred.

What also makes Clubhouse different is that it is an invitation-only site. You cannot just join the Clubhouse. A current user must invite you, or you must request an invitation from Clubhouse. When you request an invitation from Clubhouse, you may have to wait quite a while before the Admin grants it.

Why this Book?

Why do we need a book about this new application? Clubhouse is not just another social media site that happens to be audio. There are many exciting possibilities for business and marketing lurking within this application.

In this book, I will teach you what Clubhouse is all about and how to navigate it. I will then discuss the opportunities for business and marketing plans. My goal to give you the tools you need to get your invitation and jump on board Clubhouse as soon as possible. To use Clubhouse to increase your brand recognition and customer base is a primary goal.

Chapter two will introduce you to Clubhouse and its history. Just what is this new social media site? In Chapter Three, I will discuss how to get the app and get approval to join. Getting off to a fast start, setting up your profile, and navigating the app are the subjects of Chapters Four and Five.

Beginning with Chapter Six, I will get into the guts of the application and what you will experience as you navigate it. Chapter six covers the “hallway” when you first enter the app. Chapters 7-8, respectively, will cover Clubhouse Rooms, Clubhouse Stages and Clubhouse Clubs.

In chapter 9, I will discuss some of the case studies from the Clubhouse app. Then in Chapters 10 and 11, I will discuss the benefits and the pitfalls of doing business on Clubhouse. How do you use this app for business, and what pitfalls can you avoid by knowing about them in advance?

Chapter Twelve will tell a few stories of actual users without identifying them. In this chapter, I will also discuss the use of Clubhouse by a wide variety of celebrities. Finally, in the conclusion in Chapter 13 I will review and look at what makes Clubhouse right for you or not right for you.

This app is free, and I think you will find it is quite valuable. You will have to decide how it can help you best, but the possibilities are certainly there. I will discuss how you might grow your brand or network through Clubhouse. There are also many events you can join as well.

One disclaimer I must make at this point is that since Clubhouse is such a new application, it is quite possible that some of the things I present here could change. As you read through this book remember that the app could change how you download it, where you get it, setting up your profile and entering rooms. Everything is subject to change as the application is still in the Beta stage. For now I have laid out the app just as it is.

So, come along on this journey, exploring one of the most unique and fascinating social media applications to come along in a very long time.

Not since the early days of My Space and The Facebook have, we seen this kind of creativity and interest in a new social media app.

"Over the Shoulder"
STEP-BY-STEP
Training Videos

To get access visit:

ClubhouseTraining.APP

Chapter Two:
What is this New Social Media Site called Clubhouse?

Just what is the Clubhouse app, and from where did it appear on the internet? As I mentioned in the introduction, Clubhouse is a new social media app and a new kind at that. While we have all been confined by COVID-19, many of us have missed our social interactions. This is especially true of just under 30% of Americans working from home.

Yes, we have all been "zooming" for meetings, family gatherings, and even religious services. Still, it was not quite enough. For both personal and business reasons, the Clubhouse application was born. In the Clubhouse, all discussions are audio-only – no texting or tweeting. In the Clubhouse, one can discuss almost anything. There are discussions about the state of the country, political news, social movements, artistic TED type discussions, and business issues.

The advantage that the Clubhouse founders believe they have discovered is that with a voice-only social site, the participant does not need to be paying attention to their video screen. You can participate in Clubhouse while cooking dinner, driving home, or walking the dog.

You can be listening and participating in any of a myriad of topics, each in their own discussion "room."

What is Clubhouse?

When you open the Clubhouse app, you will see that you are in a hallway and can choose from many different chat rooms. You can enter anyone you want, and each room will have a specific topic of conversation. However, within each room, the conversation may veer off in any direction that the people in the room take it. I will discuss rooms in more detail in Chapter 7. You can raise your hand to speak in any room or create your room. The speakers on the "stage" in each room decide who gets to talk by recognizing you if you raise your hand.

In the Clubhouse, you can meet with friends and just hang out, or you can meet new friends from all over the world. Most of us have experienced this with Facebook, Instagram, and/or Twitter. The difference for Clubhouse lies in two aspects. The first is, of course, the voice-only application that lets you participate almost anywhere at any time. The second aspect is surprising and has added significantly to the popularity of the site. This second aspect is the presence on the site of many well-known celebrities like Oprah or TDE Rapper Reason.

You should also know two other very specific things about the Clubhouse. First, it is an iPhone only application at this time. It is written only in the Apple operating system. Secondly, it is an invitation-only application. You cannot just join it. You must be invited. This invitation-only status is also a big part of its attraction to so many people. It just might be the most "social" of all social media once you get in.

We all know how easy it is for any of us to misinterpret someone else's written communication. This misunderstanding happens because we cannot see them, nor can we hear them. With Clubhouse, you can hear the person you are having a discussion with. You have access to their tone of voice and inflection. You can hear the emotion in their voice. You cannot do this with Facebook or Twitter. Clubhouse is a more direct human connection like video conferencing, except you can do it in your pajamas. No one will see you. Sympathy and empathy come across in the voice in ways it cannot with written text.

Clubhouse is a place where you can talk for hours or minutes. People come back time after time because they deepen their relationships each time they meet. The founders of this application describe it in this way. "Clubhouse is "a new type of social product based on voice that allows people everywhere to talk, tell stories, develop ideas, deepen friendships, and meet interesting new people around the world."

Clubhouse is more like a podcast where you can have a free-flowing discussion than any other social media. You can start out talking to one group of people and end up having dropped in on multiple conversations while you are there. It could be similar to a business cocktail party or Chamber of Commerce after hours. Or it could be like a house party with all your friends and different groups of friends discussing sports in one corner, food in another, and politics on the deck.

There are book clubs and discussion groups on how people deal with the pandemic or new car prices. You can either engage in the conversation or just listen if you do not feel like talking. In many users' minds, the Clubhouse app is in many ways, just like real-life interactions.

Where did Clubhouse Come From?

In 2000 Paul Davidson and Rohan Seth developed the app and set up shop. Soon they had 1500 users and a value of about one hundred million dollars. There was a buzz in the tech world about the app. Soon celebrities like Chris Rock and Van Jones were hopping on board. This much excitement for a program still in beta and requiring an invitation to join? This much buzz for an app that is not yet open to the general public. Seth and Davison developed Clubhouse, and a venture capital company, owned by Andreessen Horowitz, financed it. Davison and Seth created a parent company for Clubhouse – Alpha Exploration Company.

Much like Twitter, you can find others in the Clubhouse app and follow them whether you know them or not. Once the conversation is finished, it disappears. There is no record or tape of the talks.

Most users would say it is a very good thing as the discussions can get quite heated at times.

This past May, there were 3500 users, and the app can have 10,000. The key is to get invited to join. Needing an invitation will be true as long as the app is still in the beta stage. Even though the app is still new, still in beta, and actually a niche type program, it's quick rise shows a real desire for this type of social media.

Part of the appeal is that it is invitation only, and there are not many invitations given out each day. Only about 10-12 invitations are offered. On any given day, at any given time, you will find around 270 users chatting. Also interesting is how both Davidson – one of the creators – and Horowitz – the venture capitalist – are often found in one of the chat rooms. Davidson is usually seeking real-time feedback from the users.

Some of the quick success of Clubhouse can be attributed to the pandemic and how much time we are spending in our homes, away from friends and staring at screens. There is a need for chat groups to replace in-person interactions. Many of us are tired of staring and screens and would like to do something else while visiting with friends. Just like you would if they were sitting in your kitchen while you fixed a meal.

Twitter requires screen time. TikTok can be confusing. Other social media sites such as Twitch, Youtube, Facebook, LiveStream, and Instagram all have their place and might not quite being what you want. Clubhouse gives your hands and eyes-free voice chat on just about any subject you want to discuss and with a wide variety of friends, professionals, celebrities, and those who just want to listen.

If TED talks had question and answer or discussion sessions throughout the talk – they would be a lot like what Clubhouse offers. Yet, unlike many other internet social media sites, it is not a free for all. The room moderator gets to decide who can speak, and you are muted until recognized to speak. There is no one talking over anyone else. In the tech world of Silicon Valley, having an invite to Clubhouse is s reason to brag. In this world of entrepreneurs and creators, social media is unusual for a social media site to generate the kind of noise that Clubhouse is making. In this tech start-up world, few programs survive, no less thrive as a beta site like Clubhouse is doing. However, if you make it, there are billions of dollars to be made for the first investors and the developers. Just think of the billions generated by the likes of Facebook, Snap, Twitter, Pinterest, Instagram, and LinkedIn.

The money made in this field is made from advertisers and based on the number of users and growth of users. Most advertising of the social media app is by word of mouth. How did you get started on Facebook? Do you even remember Friendster or My Space? Younger generations will never have heard of the sites that do not own their field. How will Clubhouse make money? That is still to be seen.

Most new start-ups in social media end up being fads that last a season or so. It's either feast or famine in this business.

You either make it big or fail. The jury is still out on Clubhouse, but it has all the makings of a successful venture. Will it survive once the pandemic is over, and we all go back to work in offices and retail?

Once we can have real house parties, watch the game together or hang out at the water cooler, will Clubhouse still have the same appeal? Right now, it is a great place to socialize in real-time and the closest thing to really "hanging out." It's easy to use, fun to navigate, and remember the no hands, no eyes appeal. It is, at the moment, the virtual hot spot for Silicon Valley's socializing. It does not hurt that Oprah, Drake, and many other celebrities love the app and use it often.

Where could you walk into a house party and engage Oprah in conversation? Where could you pitch your own entrepreneurial to billion-dollar venture capitalists?

So, let us review. Clubhouse is a social media platform for real-time, online chatting, discussion, and networking using a voice-only application. In the next few chapters, I will discuss the format for using the app. You can chat in a variety of rooms or start your own. You can create your own club. You can talk about anything you want.

Currently, this is an invitation-only social media chat site, and that exclusivity has created a larger market of people who want in. Celebrities and millionaires could be in the same room with you.

It is hands-free and screen-free, and it is the internet's version of a house party. It is also an iPhone only app. Android users are out in the cold for the time being. It is the intent of the developers to move the platform from beta to a public site and develop software for Android users. You can join a discussion while cooking dinner, doing the laundry, or just relaxing in your favorite chair. There is no need to think about what you are wearing or if you have had a haircut since the pandemic started.

Will it last? Will celebrities drop in when the app is open to the general public, and the exclusivity is gone? All of that remains to be seen. Now is the time to get on board and take advantage of the marketing, networking, and branding opportunities that are currently available.

Chapter Three:
Getting the Clubhouse App and Joining

Are you intrigued yet? Do you want to try out and explore this new gathering place? Well, good luck because part of the Clubhouse charm is its exclusivity. At the moment, you need an invitation to join the fun. The creators of Clubhouse consider it to be in the Beta stage. The final product will be open to the public, but you need an invitation for now.

Downloading the App

Anyone can download the application, but that will not get you in the door. The developers, Paul Davison, and Rohan Seth are limiting access to 10,000 users in the Beta stage. That is actually good news as there is over 600,000 users right now. There is plenty of space for more users if you can get invited.

Another essential factor is Clubhouse is only available to iPhone users. There will be an Android version, but it does not exist yet. You may have heard the buzz around this application.

It is not probably that you have joined the app. Want into Clubhouse. Get yourself an invitation to this currently exclusive club.

Want to try it out, and you are an iPhone user? Go to the Apple Appstore or the Google Play site and download the Clubhouse app. This is the Beta version of Clubhouse you will be downloading. What is a Beta app? It is the first version of the software that the developers release to some part of the public. Reserve your username -it can only be changed once so think it out.

The intent is for those who access the Beta software to test it and allow the developers to get any bugs out that users discover. This user group for Beta software is in some way a limited group so that the testing can be controlled. For Clubhouse, this is why it is currently an invitation-only application. So, you can download the app any time. You can't join the Clubhouse without an invitation.

How to Get an Invitation

There are two ways to get an invitation to join the Clubhouse. The first thing you want to do is download the application to your iPhone. Then reserve a username with the site. If you do not secure your username, someone else might just come along behind you and take your choice of name.

Once you have downloaded the app and reserved your username, you now have to get your invitation.

Again, there are two ways to do this.

1. Once you are on the waiting list with your reserved username, you just wait for the app administrator to send you an invitation. Clubhouse gives out between 10-12 invitations a day. That may seem like a lot, but with hundreds, maybe thousands on the waiting list, it really is not. So, once you get your invitation from the site, use it.
2. The other way to get an invitation is to know someone already on the site and convince them to give you an invitation. It is important to know and remember that the members do not have an unlimited number of invitations to give out.

When you are invited and join, you will receive one invitation to extend to anyone you would like. When the person you invite joins the site, you will get another three invitations. So, each member eventually has up to four invitations. You have to earn the three extra invitations by your participation and moderating of rooms.

It is usually harder to get a friend to let you in than it is to stay on the waiting list until the site invites you. You can see why this is such an exclusive site. You will receive an invitation text from either the site or your friend. It is important to remember that if you get an invitation from a friend and have not reserved a username, you cannot join. You must reserve the username first.

Just a side note: if you do not have an invitation you can speed up the process when you reserve your username.

If you have friends or business associates already in Clubhouse, they will be notified that you have reserved your username.

When they get that notification, they will be able to let you in even if they have no invitations left to send out. If they do have invitations to use, letting you through when they see your username does not use up one of those invitation.

However, when they complete their Beta testing, the plan is to go public as a free site. Going public will include offering an application for the Android operating system as well. The developer/owners want to move slowly to be sure the site can handle a large influx of users and that the interest in the site can be maintained without the exclusivity.

As it says on the Clubhouse site: *"We are building Clubhouse for everyone and working to make it available to the world as quickly as possible."* The developers are looking for quality, not quantity. It is important not to lose that quality as more people join the site. Clubhouse is a relationship dependent site, so the developers do not want to endanger established relationships by letting too many people join too soon.

You can see the site is currently minimal, with only about 600,000 registered members. That might seem like a lot until you compare it to the global numbers for Facebook or Twitter.

If you do not want to wait for either of these ways to get an invitation, you might try one other thing. There is no guarantee that it will work but try adding #Clubhouse to your posts on other social media sites. It is also true that if you already have a lot of acquaintances on the app, then when you reserve your username, the app will recognize that you are friends with a bunch of other users. It is likely to offer you an invitation faster than it will someone who does not know anyone on the site.

Remember, when you first download the application and reserve your username, give it some thought. You can change your username but ONLY ONCE. After that you can never change it again.

Who is in the Clubhouse?

One of the biggest reasons for the early popularity of the Clubhouse application is the presence of celebrities, CEOs, other professionals, technical developers and pros, and entrepreneurs. The exclusivity, along with the elite members, only attracts more elite members as well as ordinary folks like us.

Who are you likely to meet in a room in the Clubhouse? The most famous person you might run into is Oprah. You might imagine the prestige that came to the site when Oprah joined. She is not a member in name only. She might drop into any discussion going on at any time.

Not really enticed by Oprah. You might run into Ashton Kutcher or Drake. Drop into a room, and Chris Rock or Kevin Hart might be there. Go to a room discussing music, and you will find rappers, songwriters, and more. If networking and business are your reason for joining

Clubhouse, then drop into several business or marketing-oriented rooms. You will find CEOs, CFOs, Marketing professionals, and top industry leaders. In fact, despite celebrities' presence and the variety of discussions, business networking is the leading reason people seek out that invitation.

If you are into politics, laws, constitutionality, or system reform, you will find those rooms as well. They are also likely to be populated by experts and top professionals in those fields. Activists will be there, along with political commentators. Clubhouse has seen discussions with Shaka Senghor, DeRay McKesson, or Van Jones.

So, the question remains – will the site be as popular when it goes public? Will the celebrities, entrepreneurs, and titans of industry and capital still be there? Will the rooms become too crowded for the personal discussion that is the heart of Clubhouse? Only time and opening up the site can answer these questions.

I will discuss rooms in more detail in a future chapter, but if you enter a room where a discussion is in progress, there is no way to know what was discussed before you entered the room.

There is no record of the discussion kept anywhere. You might also enter a room with one discussion title and find that the conversation has veered off into an entirely different direction. At that point, you can stay or find another room. Just remember there are no rules. There are moderators, but the room is basically monitoring itself.

Other conversations that have occurred in the Clubhouse include:

- MC Hammer's discussion of rap's history and future. You might also find MC discussing the impact of Covid 19 on prison populations. This discussion also included Shaka Senghor, Van Jone, Ben Horowitz, Marc Andreessen, and venture capitalists.
- In another room, you will find Ben Horowitz again, along with Hip hoppers and rappers. Fab 5 Freddy was there along with Jared Leto and Kevin Hart. Horowitz hopes to recruit new talent to bring to the Clubhouse.
- Marketing Influencers: Frank Kern, Joseph McClendon, Dean Graziosi, Rich Schefren, Perry Belcher, Kevin Harrington, and the list goes on...
- There are many technical discussions with current and past employees of Google, Microsoft, and others. There have been very serious discussions such as the "realities of being a Black man in America today."
- There is a group of the first hundred or so users that meets every night and stay up talking till 4 in the morning. They talk about anything but tech.
- You might find Kanye West, Estelle, Meek Mill or Tiffany Haddish in deep discussion with entrepreneurs from Silicon Valley in another room.

So now you have registered your username and accepted your invitation. What comes next? How do you really get started? Let's go to Chapter four and find out.

"Over the Shoulder"
STEP-BY-STEP
Training Videos

To get access visit:

ClubhouseTraining.APP

Chapter Four:
Getting started on Day One

Now that you have accepted the invitation and have your username, it's time to log in and get started. It's time to shake off the pandemic blues or sheltering in place and not visiting with friends. Joining Clubhouse now gives you access to the typical office or home party without the introverts' social awkwardness. No one will see you. They will only hear you, and that makes it more comfortable to jump into conversations with strangers.

Are you familiar with Houseparty – a social network site where you can just join in conversations at random? Clubhouse is the audio version of the video program called Houseparty. Both apps allow spontaneous conversations with strangers and friends.

So, what do you see when you download the app to get started? You will be greeted by – a blank screen. Yes, that is right, a blank screen. Just be patient, however, and a Clubhouse member will explain to you how the application works. This person will walk you through all the different actions and options you have on Clubhouse.

This member will explain to you that when you first enter Clubhouse, you are in a hallway. From this hallway, you will be able to eventually enter any room or club that you either belong to or want to join. However, the first time you enter Clubhouse, you will initially join a large "global" type of room and join your first discussion.

You can listen only or request to talk. How you request to speak will be discussed in detail in Chapter Seven. At the same time, when you open the application, everyone on the app will be notified that you have joined. Now they can join you in any chat they wish to.

In the next chapter, I will discuss in detail how to set up your profile and navigate the app. In the remainder of this chapter, I will explain just a few of the actions and tools that are available to you on your first day in Clubhouse. Be prepared for your online experiences to change from day one of your membership in Clubhouse.

Here are a few other things you need to know. Even as Clubhouse opens your world up to conversations with buddies, celebrities, or venture capitalists, it also requires something from you. Do not be a bully and help to develop the ethics and etiquette of the site. If you want to keep enjoying Clubhouse, you will need to actively assist its growth in this area. The controversy surrounding Clubhouse has been due to their lack of tight regulations about hate speech.

There have been some discussions and sessions that have come under extreme criticism for racism and antisemitism. It is up to the members to push for more stringent rules and consequences for such behavior.

Features of Clubhouse

So, you have entered the application, and you are in the hallway. Here you can see all the rooms that are currently open. There will be a menu on the top bar and a bottom bar that allows you to start your own room. The top-line menu will tell you what events are scheduled in the future.

Member Search

There is a Member Search icon on the top left of the page. Here you can look up other members, whether by the username or by searching for keywords in their profile. For the most part, this would require you to know the person you are trying to find. However, some celebrities and professionals might be found by searching for their real names, such as "Oprah" or "Jay-Z."

- Tap on the member search icon.
- A page will come up that says: "People to Follow" and a search box that says: "Search by Keyword."
- You can use any keyword you chose. When you do this, the program will search in user-profiles and by the username to find who you want. You could use a topic as a keyword, like rap music, anything that would help you find the member.
- A list of members will come up, and you will see if the person you are looking for is there. You will

also see next to each username a button labeled Follow. Tap this for any of the users and start following them just as you would on Twitter or Facebook.

Invitation System

Now you can add your friends to the invitation system. Remember you will get one invitation when you join and can earn up to three more. But you will want to add friends' emails so that if they appear in the log on, you can be notified and let them in.

Notifications

The notifications section is where you will see items of interest to you, such as being friended by other members and events your friends have scheduled.

Calendar

There is a calendar of upcoming scheduled events you might want to attend. Put these on your personal schedule. Click on the calendar icon you will see a list of events. They will look like this:

Title of Event **Date and Time of Event**

You will see a greenhouse icon, and if you tap this, it will tell you if a specific club is a host for this event. You will also see a short description of the event and the names and pictures of the hosts of this event.

Now tap on the title line for the event. You will get a new screen and be able to choose from several options. You can:

- Share the Event with your contacts. This tab gives you an iOS widget to share the link in messaging applications and texts. Remember, you cannot send this widget to an Android user. Clubhouse is an iPhone only application.
- Copy Link will allow you to post the URL on other sites.
- Tweet a prewritten announcement about the event with a link to the event.
- Add to Cal will let you send the event information to any other scheduling applications you might use. Remember, you will also see these upcoming events at the top of the page when you enter the hallway. You will also receive notifications on events from people you are following.

Anyone can add events to this calendar. You will also see on this page an + icon in the top right corner. When you tap on this + icon, you will be able to create your own event. You will need to enter:

- The Name of the event as you want it to show in the calendar.
- Add another Host, Co-Host, or Guest Host to your event. Your username will automatically be associated with the event.
- Tap on Date/Time, and you will get a drop-down menu to select the exact date and time of the event.

- If there is a Club that this event is part of, then tap on the Host Club button. A list of all the Clubs where you are permitted to create events in their rooms.
- Hit the Description tab and write a short but enticing description of your event.
- At the top right, you will see a button to Publish. Tap on this, and your event will be published to the calendar. The event will then appear in Upcoming Events at the top of the hallway page.

This completes your initial activities on day one of the app. Here is an example of what you might find if you enter a discussion on day one. Pick a room. It might be your friends or a topic. You might find ordinary people in the room, or you might discover titans of whatever industry you are discussing. You will probably hear stories and gain insights into that topic that you might never see anywhere else. You will feel like you are sitting around a table at the bar, listening to experts in this field talk for hours with each other. You will want to spend time with people who are succeeding at your passions – doing better than you are. You will want to learn from the rooms you spend time in.

What will strike you is how "real" these discussions are – how passionate they might become. You will hear meaningful, intense discussions or just silly barroom talk.

If you are intrigued by what one person is saying, or you might want to talk with that person, you can follow them, see what other rooms they are in, or invite them to a room you create.

So just join the app and wait for your invitation. Remember to choose a username you want to live with as you can only change it once. Start by following people you find to be amazing and awesome in the areas you are interested in. Check out the rooms the people you are following are in. Listen to these incredibly successful people for a few minutes or a few hours.

The room you join might have from 10 to 300 people. They are all there for the same reason you are – to have a great conversation and learning experience.

See who will network with you offsite as well. Go to their profiles and follow them to offsite locations like Twitter, Instagram, Linked-In and more. When you contact them off site, refer back to your conversation on Clubhouse. Remember, Clubhouse is still an invitation only app. The fact that you are a member opens a lot of doors with more well-known or celebrity members. Listen in on a "million-dollar room" where all the speakers are millionaires. See what you can learn from them in the room and possible off the app.

Profile

Now let's move to chapter five, build your profile, and begin to navigate through the rest of the app. I will detail specifics about rooms, stages, and clubs in the upcoming chapters. Then I will turn my attention to how you can use Clubhouse for your business and how it can benefit you.

Chapter Five:
Setting Up Your Profile & Navigating the App

If you are going to join Clubhouse and get the most out of your time there, then this is a very important chapter. Without a profile, you cannot get started even after you are invited.

Building on your introduction to the application in the last chapter, it is time to build your profile. If there is any repetition of information between these chapters, it is because the information is important. I want to make sure you clearly understand it.

Enter the app, and you find yourself in the hallway, as discussed in Chapter Four. You will also find the profile on the top menu bar where you found the member search, invitations, calendar, and events. The last icon in the menu bar will say profile. The same basic information is displayed in everyone's profile. There are still some categories that you can edit and personalize.

Everyone's profile contains this same basic information, to begin with. Each profile contains:

- A picture which you can change anytime you like. You can upload an image from your phone. Try to make sure it is a picture that looks good no matter what size it is. Once you upload your picture to your profile, it will show up in various places throughout the app, in different sizes, with or without your name. Try to find a picture with a bright background. So be happy with the world seeing the image you upload.
- Full name followed by your username.
- Number of people you are following.
- Number of people following you.
- Profile information that you can edit at any time. Make sure that the information that you most want others to know is upfront. The first three sentences will appear as a preview in the rooms you visit (with your picture). Get the most important information in those three sentences. You have about 125 characters to work with.
- When writing this, think about what you have to offer to the conversation. This profile is not a resume, but it is a marketing tool to get others to want a conversation with you. You might also note in this section the kinds of things you are interested in discussing. If you want this profile info to be formatted or want to use emojis, you can write it in another application like Notes and copy/paste it back into Clubhouse. You cannot use live links in this section of Clubhouse.
- Links to your Twitter and Instagram accounts.
- The date you joined Clubhouse and who invited you.

Most of this information is self-explanatory, but the most important item is probably the profile biographical information.

The more information you enter here, the easier it will be for others to find you. This section needs to include the keywords that others would use to search for your profile.

This section will also show others the names of any clubs that you belong to. Take your time completing this information. If your friends know you well as a huge NFL fan and a specific team fan, put that in your profile bio.

If you are a musician, software developer, or author, be sure those keywords show up here.

For instance, do not say "I wrote this book" if your friends are likely to use the keyword author. Instead, say something like "I am the author of 5 books" and list the books' names. Once you have completed your profile take a look at the settings of the application.

Settings

In the profile, you will see an icon that looks like "gear." Tap on this, and you will see the list of settings along with other information. Let's take a look at what you can choose in the Settings.

Notifications

First, you will see the settings for notifications. You can decide how often you want to receive notifications and the type of notifications. With respect to how often you get notifications, you can choose from:

- Very Frequent
- Frequent
- Normal
- Infrequent
- Very Infrequent

You can also pause notifications in effect, turning them off.

You can also choose "Include Trending Rooms" so you will receive notifications about the most popular rooms.

Information and Links

Next, in settings, you will see a section on additional information and external links.

These included:

- What's New – this Tab gives you information regarding any changes to the application through updates. The update is named and followed by a list of whatever changes the new update included.
- FAQ/Contact Us – This is a link to the Help Center for Clubhouse. Here you will find a Frequently Asked Section and a way of submitting your own questions or feedback. You can also submit questions for an online Weekly Town Hall held on Sundays at 9 a.m. PT.
- Next, in the settings, you have a tab for Report an Incident – this takes you to a form to fill out regarding a problem you are having. This form goes to the Trust and Safety team. For instance, if you

are in a room that is getting racist and disrespectful to some people in the room, you can report this.

- The next Tab is Community Guidelines. Hit this Tab, and it will give you the Clubhouse Code of Conduct.
- The next Tab gives you the Clubhouse Terms of Service – If you are not a lawyer, you might not have much interest in this. It's there if you want it.
- The next Tab in Settings is the Privacy Policy, much like the privacy policy every website has.
- The final section in Settings is Other Social Media. Here you can link your Clubhouse application to your Twitter, LinkedIn, and Instagram accounts. Once you connect these links to your other social media accounts will appear in your profile. Now your friends can jump from your Clubhouse account to your Twitter account. The same is true for LinkedIn and Instagram.

Clubhouse will allow you to automatically add who you follow to your phone's contacts. You can also choose the topics you want to follow/discuss. Based on your history of entering discussion rooms and the people and topics you follow; the app will suggest other people or issues you might choose to follow.

When the app recommends people for you to follow, you will see a list called "Find Conversations About...". You can then choose the topics you are most interested in. You can be general or specific in the topics you choose. You do this by selecting a category like Sports. Once you choose this category, another list will appear, offering you more specific choices such as basketball, Olympics, American football, and more. You can do this with all the topics you see listed under "Find Conversations About."

Just to give you an example of a few of the more than 140 topics for selection in the profile settings here are a few:

- World Affairs
- Sports
- Current U.S. Politics
- Wellness
- Entertainment
- Music
- Arts
- Faith
- Tech
- Hustle
- Hanging Out

Your bio on your profile should give others a pretty good idea of what topics might be important to you.

Once you have completed your profile and your Settings choices, you can move on to navigate the rest of the Clubhouse application. You return to the hallway and choose a room to enter or a club to join. Perhaps you want to create your own club or start a room. How do you do these things?

The following chapters will answer this question in detail. You might notice some repetition with items in previous chapters. I have briefly touched on these topics in the first five chapters. Now I will discuss them in detail.

Chapter Six:
Clubhouse Hallway

Welcome to the shortest chapter of the book. This chapter is short because the Clubhouse Hallway, though very important, does not require very much explanation. The Hallway is where you land whenever you open the application after your first time. Remember the first time you are greeted by a Clubhouse member and given a tour of the app.

It is in the Hallway that you will get access to rooms where discussions are going on. If you have already followed some rooms, you will see tabs for those here. Any clubs you have joined will show up in the Hallway as well. These will show up on the top of the Hallway.

On the top of the Hallway page, there is the Main Menu. As reviewed in detail in Chapter 5, you can access many features from the main menu. To review this menu allows you to:

- Send invitations to others to join the Clubhouse. You will see how many invitations you have available to send. If someone wants to join through you, they must send you a text on your iPhone. Before this, you need to grant access to your phone contacts to Clubhouse. Then when you want to invite someone, you can look through this list and choose someone. They will get a text inviting them to join Clubhouse.

Other actions you can perform from the Hallway Main Menu were covered in Chapter Five. These included:

- Search for members through name or keywords.
- See the calendar and upcoming rooms and events.
- Check your notifications.
- Edit your Clubhouse profile.

The most important and most used function in the Hallway will be your access to the rooms you want to enter for discussion. Want a bunch of diversity in the rooms you see in the Hallway? The way to get more variety is to add more followers and get more people to follow you.

Jargon or the Talk of the Clubhouse

Many social media sites have their own shortcuts in language or use emojis a lot. There is jargon in the Clubhouse as well. Here are the three most important pieces of jargon that you need to know.

- Stages – when you enter a room, you will find some people on "stage" and others in the "audience," so to speak. The people on stage are usually the ones who started the room and started the discussion. Members of the audience are either followed by the speakers or follow them. Then some people randomly entered the room and are not followed or following the speakers.

- Moderator – This person leads the discussion. Moderators are in charge of who can be on stage. They can let you on or kick you off. They also have the power to mute you or to send you out of the room entirely. If you want to speak, you raise your hand, and the moderator may or may not call on you. You raise your hand by tapping on that icon. It is the moderator's job to keep the discussion within bounds and let as many people speak as possible.
- Host Moderator – This person "opens" the room. Once the other moderators are named, the host has no more influence or power than any other moderator. If necessary, another moderator can even remove the host moderator from the room.
- "PTR" – This means "pull to refresh," which means the moderator wants to reset the room. This happens when the number of people in the room is high, and there is too much passion or some disrespect from speakers. When a moderator yells out "PTR," they are attempting to regain control of the room.

In the next chapter, I will discuss rooms, stages, and moderators in detail.

"Over the Shoulder"

STEP-BY-STEP

Training Videos

To get access visit:

ClubhouseTraining.APP

Chapter Seven:
What happens in a Clubhouse room?

When you are standing in the Clubhouse Hallway, you can see a listing of all the rooms that are available for you to enter and jump into a discussion. You can start your own room or choose from all the rooms available to you in the Hallway.

You can choose to join one of these rooms or decide to start your own. In order to do either, you need to understand how rooms work and what rules you will need to follow.

Rooms

When you enter the Hallway and look around, you can choose from many rooms and discussions. Once you select the room and conversation you want to join; you simply enter the room. You do this by clicking on Don't be nervous when you first enter the room. You will be muted, and you can unmute yourself. If you choose just to listen, you will never have to be unmuted or speak.

However, if you do wish to speak, you can raise your hand and be recognized if the room moderator chooses to recognize you.

When you first enter the room, what will the setup be? There will be a stage and an audience. Picture "break out rooms" at a large convention. That is what many of these Clubhouse rooms are like. At the same time, you might find a room that is more like the general session at a convention with hundreds of participants in the room.

While you are still in the Hallway, before you enter a room, you can see the title of the discussion, who is in the room in terms of the number of people, a list of who some of those people are, and who the speakers are. If you can see this about a room while you are in the Hallway, then it is either a room with a speaker you are following or a public room. Anyone can enter a public room.

If there are specific people you want to meet in a room or a particular discussion you wish to join, you can check by swiping left while in the Hallway. You will then see a list of everyone online and where they are.

Seeing all the rooms you have access to requires that you scroll the rooms. Scroll down to see all the rooms available to you. Scroll back up to find the one you want to join. It is important to note though, that not all rooms on the platform will show up in your Hallway. They do not show up because you do not have access to every room.

There are many private rooms, and there are many rooms that do not fit the topics you said you were interested in your profile when you wrote your profile. This first set of rooms also must have someone you are following or someone who is following you in the room. The application algorithm will decide what rooms you can see.

As previously mentioned, each room will display the name of the room, the name of the club is any, and a list and numbers of the number and names of those in the room. Again, you will not see the names of everyone in the room. You will only see the speakers and audience members who are in your network. You will know how many speakers there are and how many people are in the audience.

If you scroll all the way to the end, you will find an "Explore" command with an image of the world as the icon. If you tap on this command, you will get even more rooms that you can explore. These "explore" rooms are those from the followers of your followers.

Now let me explain how the stage, speakers, moderators, and audience work.

Stage

The Stage is where the speakers are. This group might include the person who opened the room, experts who were invited to the room, the moderators, and anyone the moderator(s) allows on the stage.

The state is the first thing you see when you enter a room. Near the top of your page -top of the room – you have the person who created the room, moderators, and speakers. Everyone in the room who wishes to speak must be on the stage. Those on the stage take turns when they want to talk.

Underneath the speakers is the audience. The first few rows are people who are "followed by the speakers." This section is labeled as such. This section of users already has an initial relationship with the speakers. Below this section is the rest of the audience. This is everyone else who came into the room to listen.

Everyone on stage will have their name and profile displayed along with their picture. IF they recently joined Clubhouse, they might have an emoji as well. This area will also tell you if the person on the stage is muted or not. When someone on the stage speaks, a line around their profile will light up, so you know who is speaking. Anyone on the stage with an icon of a green stat is a room moderator.

Speakers

So, you entered a room with a topic you are very interested in and with people who follow you. When you first enter, you are a member of the audience, and you are muted. If you follow any of the speakers on stage, you will be placed in the first section of the audience. If you wish to speak, you raise your hand by clicking on the hand button on your screen. The moderator might or might not recognize you. That choice is entirely up to the moderator. If you are recognized, then you are asked to the stage to speak. You cannot talk unless you are on the stage.

Once you are on the stage, you can mute or unmute yourself as you wish. Most rooms ask speakers to keep their microphones muted out of courtesy to the person who is speaking. If you are speaking, you will re-mute yourself when you are done.

However, there might be a slight delay from the time you stop speaking to everyone having heard you. So, do not mute yourself too quickly.

However, keeping your mic muted while you are on the stage is important for keeping the background noise down.

A few more things for speakers to remember. If you are answering questions keep your answers concise depending on the number of speakers and audience members in the room. If there are a lot of people in the room, make your answers short and concise. Keep the conversation moving. Do not get bogged down in a lot of technical talk unless the only people in the room are techies.

Do not try to sell from the stage if you are a speaker. This is not a sales forum. You can make a lot of money through Clubhouse but directly pitching from the stage is not how it's done. This is frowned upon. Give your audience the value they want, and they will follow you off app. If you attempt to sell you will be greeted with a lot of discontent and grumbling.

Unless you are the only speaker on the stage in a keynote type setting, do not try to answer every question. Give other speakers a chance to answer as well.

Finally, you can PING top influencers and celebrities and invite them to your room to speak. If they agree then all of their followers will receive a notification that they are in your room. Your room can fill up quickly if this happens.

So, with all the power, they seem to have in the rooms, let's take a look at the moderators.

Moderators

As I've discussed above, the moderator of a room has plenty of control over what happens in the room. A strong moderator might run a room that allows for full discussion and participation by anyone who wants to talk. A weaker moderator can lose control of a room and end up with an angry and chaotic discussion. So, the role of the moderator is the most critical in the room.

How does one get to be a moderator in any room? There are basically two ways to do this.

1. Create and open the room yourself. You are now the owner and original moderator for your room.
2. You might be invited by a room owner to be the moderator in their room. Being a moderator is, in effect, a promotion from the role of speaker to the role of moderator. You might enter the room as an audience member and end up as the moderator.

Now that you are the moderator, you have a lot of control over the room and a choice in actions to be taken. Some of the things you can do include:

- You control the ability of the audience members to ask to speak by raising their hands. If your room will be a listening only room, you can turn off the icon for individuals to raise their hands.
- If you are allowing audience members to speak, you have a different set of choices. You can accept the individual in the audience request to speak when they raise their hands, or you can reject/ignore it.

- You can invite certain members of the audience to come up to the stage and become a speaker.
- You can mute speakers if you choose to without forcing them back into the audience.
- Force speakers to return to the audience.
- Name one or more of the speakers to take on the role of room moderator(s).

How the moderator runs her room depends on the number of people in the room and the interest in the owner and speakers. The one thing about the Clubhouse is everyone is at the mercy of the moderator(s), even the owner of the room. What tends to happen when there are a large number of people in the room, the moderator completely controls the discussion.

He will call a group of people to the stage and limit their discussion or questions to only a few minutes. He will then send the group back to the audience and bring a new group to the stage. In this way, everyone who wants to talk will get a chance to do so without verbal chaos.

The way a moderator runs a smaller group of people might be entirely different. There are no rules for how to moderator a room. If the room is small enough, the moderator(s) might invite everyone up to the stage to speak. You might see a panel type discussion in other rooms that the audience just listens to or one with time set aside for questions.

There can be different ways that moderators set up their rooms and stages.

Here are a few basics that you will see often. However, there may be moderators who choose to do them another way. Here are three basic setups.

1. One speaker = run kind of like a keynote speaker at a conference or event with questions and answers.
2. Two to five speakers = Usually set up like a conference style panel discussion with questions and answers.
3. If there are more than 5 speakers in a room the format is usually an open forum – could be a free for all if the moderator does not keep control of the room.

If the owner of the room is going to hand over moderating authority to others, it should be decided before the room is opened. Making this decision is essential so that the moderators know what is coming, set the room's tone, and determine what type of format they might be using.

Decide beforehand if your room will just be a designated group of speakers or a panel, and everyone else will just listen. At the same time, the moderator can change the rules as they go. How the moderator handles the room will have a lot to do with how the conversation flows.

The moderator or owner should decide in advance who the initial speakers are and touch base with them before the room is opened. Decide what the format will be – free flow discussion or structured discussion. Decide if the moderator will choose new speakers in a structured way or just respond to anyone who raises their hand.

Other roles the moderator will need to play includes moderating the room. As long as the room is open, the moderator must be there to control the conversation flow. When the discussion becomes passionate in a crowded room, the moderator must keep track of who is speaking and ensure that one or two people do not dominate the conversation. He needs to call on other people when this begins to happen. Another way to keep track of who is speaking is to make all speakers introduce themselves before they speak every time.

If the conversation slows down and seems to be dying, the moderator has two choices. She can change the speakers with new ones from the audience or just open the stage up to everyone. The second choice would be to acknowledge that the discussion is done and close the room.

In every situation, it is imperative that the moderator not lose control of the room or lose the interest of the audience. Never pressure anyone into speaking if they are hesitant but never let anyone monopolize the discussion. It is also the role of the moderator to keep the discussion ethical, non-abusive and prevent any bullying.

The role of the moderator is a somewhat encompassing one. So, if you are the owner of the room but do not want to moderate it, be very selective in your choice of moderator. Remember, it is your room. You opened it, and you will want the discussion in that room to deal with the specific reasons you opened it. Make sure your moderator meets your needs.

Depending upon the size of the room, the moderator might have to reset the room as often as every 10-15 minutes. To do this the moderator will review what has been said and ask everyone to PTR or Pull to Refresh. If there are speakers who have been inappropriate or hog the stage, moderators can send them back to the audience.

Moderators can block inappropriate speakers. The Clubhouse will make up a list of blocked speakers from the feedback of multiple moderators. The moderator or owner of the room can use this list to decide who the room's speakers might be.

The moderator should have an agenda even through it will be loosely followed. This is important because if the first topic peters out the moderator will be ready with a new topic. When you recognize a raised hand in the audience, move that person to the stage and unmute them. When they are finished speaking move them back into the audience. Do not let everyone stay on the stage after speaking or the stage will become too crowded, and the audience will not remember who the original panel was. Remember to remote the listener as they go back to the audience.

Audience/Listeners

When you first join the application, you do so as a listener or member of the audience. You are muted at this time with no ability to unmute. Your access at the beginning, unless you create a room, is as a listener only. It is normal for new members to listen for a while until you have a feel for the room and find yourself involved in the conversation. If you are not interested, you can "leave quietly." While listening, you can tap on any speaker or member of the audience. Tapping on a name allows you to see who is in the room with them and decide if there is anyone you want to connect with or follow.

Remember your job as a listener is to LISTEN! You might want to take notes as you are going to hear a lot of great information.

If you want to leave but are not sure where you want to go, you can scroll through the rooms while still listening in this one. Just click the "All Rooms" icon to do so. Another quirk of the Clubhouse pp is that you can minimize it and go to other apps without getting out of the room you are in. So, you can work or socialize elsewhere without losing your Clubhouse app or the room you are in. When you are ready to talk and become a speaker click on the raised hand. Now, wait or hope that the moderator will acknowledge you and bring you to the stage.

For the rest of the audience, as noted, you see the "Followed by the speakers" group first, then the other users. When you begin, you are an "other user" unless someone has specifically invited you into this room because they are a speaker, and you are following them.

Now that you understand who is in the room and their functions let's look at just what you can do once you enter a room.

Room Actions

There are several things you can do when once you are in a room. Some of these activities depend on where you are – on the stage or in the audience. You will see the action you can take at the bottom of your screen. You will only see the actions you can perform from where you are in the room.

What can you do if you are on the stage? Here are the commands available.

- Microphone – you can mute or unmute your microphone.
- Leave – simply leave the room.

What can you do when you are in the audience? Here are the commands available.

- Ping others when you see this symbol +- this means you can invite one of your followers who are not in this room to join you in this room.
- Hand Raise – Raise your hand to let the moderator(s) know you want to speak. If they recognize you, they will ask you to come to the stage.
- Leave (leave quietly) Just leave the room.

How to Start Your Own Room

The next thing you should know about rooms is how to start your own room. Remember, when you join Clubhouse, you can join existing rooms that the Clubhouse algorithm gives you or create your own room.

Creating your own room has the advantage of putting you in charge of the topic, the moderator(s), and how the group in the room socializes and interacts. When you create your own room, you will decide if it is open to the public or if you just want to talk with a few friends in a private room.

From the Hallway, you will choose Adda Topic to create your own room. The choices you will receive are Closed, Social, or Open.

- Closed – this is the private room where you want only to talk with a few friends. In addition to anyone you are following or following you, you can also "ping" others to join your private room.
- Social – this room is "kind of" private in that the only people who will be allowed in this room are people you are following or are connected in the app.
- Open- this room is what it sounds like – a room that is open to anyone who wants to come in. Again, you can ping people to join you in the room, and your followers will automatically know you have opened a room.

Then you will just need to pick the title and description of the discussion in your room. You will need to choose your speakers and moderator(s) too.

When you are in a room you will hear the moderators calling out the phrase "PTR" quite often. PTR means Pull to Refresh. This simply means that the moderators want you to refresh the screen. You do this by pulling down on your iPhone screen. The moderators will do this if there is something like a chart they want to display or new information they want to give about the room. When you Pull to Refresh you will get an update on who is currently in to room versus when you entered it. You might see different profile pictures if people change them and you will also see the order in which the audience, speakers and moderators entered the room.

Events

You can also plan events and have them put on the Clubhouse calendar. Remember when you first entered the Hallway, you had notifications and calendar tabs on the top of the page. All events that you might be interested in will be listed there.

You can add your own event to this tab. You can just enter the information and decide if your event will be hosted on simultaneous stages by your moderators or an Emcee you could hire to do so. Many people beginning to use Clubhouse for brand recognition and marketing are using events to do this. An event allows for shared rooms with multiple discussions at the same time. Almost as if you are putting together that virtual conference I alluded to earlier.

These types of events can really boost your networking and follower numbers. In these types of events, you have people sticking around for hours. The conversation is engaging, informative, and enjoyable.

There can be as many rooms with simultaneous stages as you have moderators for. This will be discussed in a future chapter on using Clubhouse to build your business.

Conclusion

As much as the Hallway is the essential entrance into the Clubhouse app, rooms are the application's primary component. Everything in Clubhouse starts with the rooms. You can spend hours sitting in a large room just listening to the conversation. If you choose to, you can go off into your own room and discuss something from the larger discussion with only one or two others. You can plan events with multiple simultaneous stages and conversations. You can join or form a club of your own. I will cover clubs in the next chapter.

"Over the Shoulder"

STEP-BY-STEP

Training Videos

To get access visit:

ClubhouseTraining.APP

Chapter Eight:
Clubhouse Clubs

In addition to stages and rooms, the Clubhouse also features Clubs. Like Rooms, Clubs are an important feature in maximizing the benefits of this application. Just as rooms are individual discussion groups or single topics, Clubs are more of a combination of discussions around a specific interest.

What are Clubs?

Members can create or join specific interest-based groups called Clubs. If you combined a Twitter group DM and a regular Facebook group, you would have something that looks like a Clubhouse Club.

If you are a Clubhouse member who wants to see if his specific interest is represented in a Club, there is no easy way to do this yet. There is a plan for a directory of Clubs, but it is not however in place. The only way at this point to find Clubs is to tap on a person you are interested in and see what Clubs they are in. This is especially effective if you know that the person you tap shares your specific interest.

Who is a Club?

Just who makes up a Club? You now know that rooms have an owner or creator, speakers, moderators, and audience members. What types of roles make up a Club?

- Founder or Administrator
- Members
- Followers
- Not a Club Follower

The Founder or Administrator of a Club has the highest level of access and permissions. This person is responsible for the description, rules, and Icon of the Club. They are also the people who can change these things. No one else can set these items or change them. The Founder or Administrator also has the permission to open rooms that are hosted by the Club. These rooms can be private or public. The Founder or Administrator also has the ability to delete members from the Club.

Members have the ability to create private Club rooms. It is not required that the Administrator do this. However, only the Members and the Administrators can see what private Club rooms are available.

Followers can only see the public rooms that a Club offers. They cannot create any spaces attached to a Club. They are notified whenever a new public room is scheduled by the Club or when the Club is hosting a public room. This notification allows the followers to always have access to the Club's public rooms.

Even if you are not a follower of a specific Club, you can still participate in the discussions in the Club's public rooms. The trick is to find out what and when Clubs are hosting public spaces because non-followers will not receive the notifications that followers do.

Finding a Club

As I previously mentioned, finding a Club is not as easy as one might think. Nor is it as easy as it should be for an application as sophisticated and popular as Clubhouse. Where you find the Clubs you follow is different from where you will find the Clubs you founded or hold membership in. To begin with, you have to go to a user's profile to find the Clubs for which they are members or founders.

At the bottom of a user's profile, there are Club icons for the clubs they founded or are members of. Remember, the Founder or Administrator sets the Icon for the Club. If the Club is created without an icon, then you will see two capital letters for the first words of the Club name. For example, if the Club Name is Future Rap, then if there is no icon you will see the capital letters "FR." Of course, this will not really help you to know what the Club is about. However, if you tap on the letters or the Icon, you will see more descriptive information about the Club. How this information is displayed and what information depends upon whether you are a founder, a member, a follower, or a non-follower.

If the user profile you are looking at is someone who follows the Club but is not a member or the Founder, the Club information will not be found here. Instead, you will have to look in this user's "Following" tab for the Clubs they follow.

Once you find the right place to look up the Club information here is what you will see based on your user status.

Non-Follower

If you are not the Club founder, member, or follower, you will only see what a non-follower sees. This includes the name and Icon of the Club, a description of the Club, and a list of members. You will only see a list of members if the Founder or Administrator has made this list public. The only button you will see on the page is the "Follow" button. Tap this if you wish to follow this Club. After doing this, you move from the non-follower's category to the Follower category.

Follower

If you are a Follower of this particular Club, the page will say "Following" instead of a Follow button. The same information that was displayed about the Club for the non-follower will be displayed for you. This includes the name and Icon of the Club, a description of the Club, and a list of members.

Member

If you are a member, you have the same options as the follower, with additional ones opened as well.

- Add Icon: You can nominate others to become members of the Club.
- Search Clubhouse: You can search all Clubhouse members and request that the ones you pick to be added to the Club. You cannot add these users to the Club membership yourself.
- Search Contacts: You can search the contacts on your iPhone and request that they be given membership into Clubhouse by being added to this Club. The Club administrators will use their invites to let your friends into Clubhouse.
- Leave the Club: tap on the three dots to bring up this option.

Founder or Administrator

Finally, the Founder or admin of a club has the most control. They can see both the members and followers of the Club. Additionally, they can set the description and Icon of the Club.

- Change the Icon – no one else can do this. Tap the Icon and then tap "change."

Tap on the Add Icon – brings up an array of new options available to the Founder/Administrator.

- Copy Secret Invite Link – You can create an invite link that allows others to join Clubhouse through your Club. These invites are not counted in your personal invites. But if you are responding to a member's request to invite their friend, the invite will show you as the inviter, not the Club member who made the request.

- Review Nominated Members: Here, you can review the nominations your Club members have made to invite new Clubhouse users or
- invite current Clubhouse members to your Club.
- Search Clubhouse: The same as the members' ability.
- Search Contacts: The same as the members' ability.

Now Tap on the quotation marks "…" to bring up even more options.

- Edit Club Rules – The Founder/Administrator is allowed to set three Club rules that your speakers coming on-stage must acknowledge and follow.
- Allow/Do not Allow Followers – You can make your Club very private by not allowing any followers.
- Let/Do not Let Members Start Rooms – You can decide whether Club members are allowed to start new private rooms with the Club as the host.
- Show/Hide Member List – Here, you decide if the Club member list is private or public.
- Edit Description – You can change the description of the Club. After the Club is open a while, you might find that your first description is not clear enough to attract members and followers.

Now that you know who can do what with Clubs, let's look at how to create the Club, to begin with.

How to Create a Club

It is essential to understand the following information. You cannot just set up a Club from within the application. To set up a Club, you must request that the Clubhouse Team do so. This is a manual process and not something that the application can just do. Remember, this is still a Beta application, and these types of things may change before the application goes public.

To request a Club:

- Go to your Profile.
- Tap on the Gear icon.
- Tap on FAQ/Contact Us.
- Scroll to "How can I start a Club?"
- Tap on the Arrow and read the Club Founder requirements.
- You will see the following message, "If all sounds good, submit your request here!" Now tap and hold on the underlined word "here."
- Tap on the "Open Link" in the preview. This gives you the form you need to complete to request a Club. You will need to provide basic information such as the name of the Club, a description of the Club, and contact information for the Founder. *Think about this carefully because once you create the Club name,* ***it cannot be changed.*** You can change the description but not the NAME.

- Once the Clubhouse Team has approved your Club, you will receive a notification on your profile. So, check it frequently.

Now, as the Founder or just a Club member, you can begin to make use of the Club. The best way to start is to go back to the Hallway and Start a Room. Now it will ask you for a topic (which is optional), and your Club will be displayed, among others. Remember, at this point; you have four choices. You can start a public, closed, or social room. Your fourth choice is to select the Club you just had created. You can name the Club room if you choose.

All Club rooms start as closed or private. It is only visible to members and will show that it is hosted by your Club. Your Club icon will be displayed. Remember, if you do not choose a Club icon, then the first letter of each of the first two words in the title or description will be displayed.

From the Hallway, you will see the name of the Club and the Icon if there is one. When you first see this, the Club will be locked, and there will be a lock symbol in the top right-hand corner. There are three dots next to the lock icon. Tap on them for your options at this point.

- Let Visitors in: This command lets you make the room public. Only the Founder or Administrator can make the room public. When you choose this, a popup will appear to ask if you are sure. Tap on your response. If you are the Founder or Administrator, you can make the room public.

- Members can also make the room public, but the name of the room and the name of the Club will not appear.
- Review Club Rules – Everyone must review the Club rules before entering the room. However, you cannot change the rules.
- Leave Club – You can simply leave the Club.

How to Schedule a Club Event

If you want to schedule a Club, you will do it the same way you would schedule a personal event. Go to the calendar from the Hallway. Add your event as described in Chapter 7 on Rooms. Before completing your event information select your Club from the list in Host Club. At this point, you can also make the event Open to Club Members Only if so desired. Members cannot make the affair public. The app is programmed to choose Open to Club Members Only unless you are the Founder/Administrator.

Once you belong to several Clubs matching your interests, your Clubhouse experience will be significantly enhanced. Clubs are great for forming tight-knit communities. Club rooms limited to members only can be very intimate and confidential in the discussions. Club events can be recurring events. If you want to introduce the Club to the full Clubhouse to get more members, this is a great way to do it.

“Over the Shoulder”

STEP-BY-STEP

Training Videos

To get access visit:

ClubhouseTraining.APP

Chapter Nine:
Is the Clubhouse Good for Business?

The next few chapters are the heart of this book. My intent is to show you how to use Clubhouse for your businesses and marketing purposes. In this chapter I will discuss if and how Clubhouse is good for your business. What are the pros and what are the cons?

In Chapter Ten, I will discuss the potential pitfalls you need to avoid while using Courthouse. Chapter Eleven shares experiences of real Clubhouse users without revealing their names. Finally, in Chapter Twelve, I will cover some examples of case studies from real users in their businesses.

I expect Clubhouse to be the next big thing in social media platforms and marketing. Yes, there are tech professionals, entrepreneurs, and celebrities on other social media platforms. People come to Clubhouse to network, for the social/party atmosphere or to make money, just like most other apps.

Clubhouse is different than those other platforms for several reasons.

The most important ones include:

- It is a voice only platform.
- It is currently invitation only.
- It has a definite FOMO (fear of missing out) factor.
- The ability to connect and discuss with professionals who are not in your specific niche or industry.
- Spontaneous conversations with real time discussions regarding just about anything.
- Instead of regurgitating other people's content like on many other platforms, here the emphasis is not on content. It is on the value of the conversation.
- Clubhouse will allow you to network, expand your knowledge, grow your credibility and authority in your field and develop creative ideas and solutions to presented issues.

Community Building

While Clubhouse is still in the Beta stage you probably won't have enough invitations to bring your whole community or clientele onto it. After the app goes public, you will be able to bring every one of your clients and your entire community into the Clubhouse. This will allow you to network within your community or client groups and between them. As you add new Clubhouse members and followers, they can interact with your networks as well. Your new Clubhouse followers will jump over to any other channels and clubs you are active with. You can easily see how you can grow your pool of potential sales or service leads.

You can invite your communities and network to your virtual events, conferences, and summits. Getting your communities to your events gives you the opportunity to interact with them in a different way and perhaps learn things you did not know. With Clubhouse you get a private, exclusive setting to hold your event within. There are no privacy concerns and no extra costs.

Your communities might even go to a live in-person event once Covid 19 is out of the way and still be able to discuss the event in virtual rooms on Clubhouse. So, while attending an in-person keynote address, you might also be discussing it in a Clubhouse room.

Building communities and networks in Clubhouse are a great way for individuals and teams to be able to collaborate on projects. Just open a private room and only invite those who will be working on the project. When your discussion is finished, you close the room and there are no notes or recordings kept. This is a great way to collaborate on a proprietary project with a team that is in different places.

Other community or network application might include:

- Podcasts – Build rooms or clubs that are related to the information on your podcast(s). Since everyone in the room will be familiar with the content of your podcast, without having any extra expenses or content generation in order to keep you audience interested and active in-between podcasts.
- Interaction with experts in various fields – One of the best things about Clubhouse is that not only can

you interact with people from your own industry, but you have the opportunity to network with experts from other industries. Imagine being able to spend hours talking with a successful entrepreneur about how to grow your business. What if you are thinking of a start up in your business or another area and could spend a day with an expert in new busines startups? What would you pay for such an experience? It's free in the Clubhouse.

What if you could spend that day with tech giants, venture capitalists or CEOs of multinational corporations or CFOs of billion-dollar companies? What would that be worth to you? Image being in the same Clubhouse room, on the same stage with these experts. Imagine asking them whatever you wanted to and getting a first-hand answer. Now add to that imagining that you also get to hear the questions and answers of another hundred people who are in the same room. Imagine the knowledge you would walk away with to put to use in your business.

Social Media Marketing

Now let's talk about how to use Clubhouse in your social media marketing. There are several ways you could do this. First, I want to say a few words about content and content creation. There is a good way to collect content for your website or other social media sites without breaking the rules of privacy in Clubhouse.

I have previously mentioned that it against the Clubhouse Terms of Use to record or transcribe anything you hear in a room, a club or at an event. Once the room is closed there is no record of the conversations that took place in that room. However, if you want to open a room to discuss how to train a dog, and you want to write an article for your website from the conversation, there is a way to do it. You need to get permission from everyone in the room in order use any of the conversations that went on in the room verbatim.

How are you going to do that without having to check with every person as they enter the room? It is not really feasible to try to do it that way. Instead, when you create your room you need to put into the public title or the room that you intend to transcribe or record the conversation. Put this in the description of your room as well.

Now anyone who enters your room knows your intentions and implicitly agrees with them. Now you can record the session, interview dog trainers, and take complete notes.

When the room is closed you can take your information and write an article for your blog or website. Just remember that you cannot change the name or description of a room once you have created the room.

So, it is very important that you set the room up this way from the beginning. You cannot be in the middle of a discussion about dog training and then decide you want to record the conversation. You must notify the participants in advance of opening the room.

Building Your Brand

This is the topic you hear most about when discussing how to use Clubhouse to advance your business. Clubhouse is still new and there is still room on the platform for a creative, imaginative businessperson to develop anything you can think of.

Over the years we have seen creative people use platforms to launch careers never thought of before. This happened with YouTube, Twitter, Instagram, and others. The same could happen on Clubhouse. You can host lounges, game nights, storytelling, talent shows, exercise events, life coaching and so much more. If you are a moderator, a speaker or a creator of a room, your opportunities to do this type of activities is endless.

No matter what you do it is critical that you are always building your brand. Let's go back to the dog trainer. If she is hosting a game night and her dog training school is called Bark-a-thon, then the game night could be Bark-a-thon's Night of Games. You could have a Bark-a-thon music night or just a Bark-a-thon Training Session.

When Clubhouse first began it was populated with techies and venture capitalists. Because of this you would find rooms where someone was pitching a new product or service to the venture capitalists or rooms where actual investments could be made. No matter what you were doing on Clubhouse you were in on the ground floor. Now the platform is a little more crowded, but you can still find these types of rooms or open one yourself. There is no better place online for a new entrepreneur to get his business financed and off the ground. There is no better place online for an experienced entrepreneur who wants to start a new line or an entirely new business. There is no better place online to discuss a career change or a complete change in your line of business.

People want more from social media going forward. They want more authentic discussions and a better feel of community. Maybe this is the result of the COVID-19 pandemic, but whatever it is, it offers you an amazing opportunity for branding and marketing. Just as search engines have come to rely on quality content, so social media sites must begin to offer users more quality discussions, transparency, and authenticity. However, they do not want to wade through all the content on most social media sites.

Let's go back to that dog trainer. She has tremendous opportunities to build her brand and market her skills. She can have a discussion with anywhere from two to hundreds in a room. She can stress her dog training experience and knowledge on her bio and include links to her Twitter and Instagram accounts. From those accounts the followers can then move to the dog trainer's website and purchase her goods and services.

The key to this is getting top notch nationally and internationally renowned speakers for whatever your specialty or business field is. Other options include holding a concert if you are a music teacher or a performer. Teachers and tutors can host a variety of children's room as can children's authors. Get parents and children in a room to hear children's stories and talk about them.

You should at least be listening in on Clubhouse if you do nothing else. This will get you ready to start promoting your brand. The time to do it is now. No one knows what kind of access you will have to the "name" speakers after the app goes public. Still the most benefits come from being a room host or a speaker. Unlike other social media the currency of Clubhouse is not content. It's conversations. If you are able to speak well, hold the interest of others and keep the conversation going, the benefits are there for the taking. The bigger your audience, the better your brand recognition.

The key is to freely share your knowledge. Like the dog trainer shares her knowledge in her room and gets her followers to follow her to her off app websites. In this environment you basically have an incubator for business and investment opportunities. A typical discussion might involve a millionaire and a billionaire, a venture capitalist, and other entrepreneurs, as well as investors.

As one of the billionaires was discussing a project with an entrepreneur, it seemed to be going nowhere. Then another investor in the room suggested another way that they could create an income stream off the original project idea. In another room one of the listeners noticed that the speakers were generating data from their business but not using it. She suggested that they could sell this data or use it to generate other income streams. So, you can see that *anything can happen,* and new ideas can come from anywhere.

Remember Kevin Harrington of *Shark Tank* fame? Well, he has been known to host rooms with thousands of participants listening to entrepreneurs pitch their products just like on the show. At the close of the room, several of the entrepreneurs had been financed and the others left with great advice.

Yet it is the collaboration rather than competition that gives Clubhouse its life. This happened because the site was initially populated by techies, entrepreneurs, artists, and entertainers. They set the culture. Then they were allowed to invite a handful of others in to join them. From there the application was allowed to grow slowly through invitation. Each new member is indoctrinated into the Clubhouse by an existing member. In this way they built and kept a very unique culture in social media. They built and kept a powerful collaborative culture where anyone can meet and talk with just about anyone else. It is indeed and incubator for business, because when you get all these high powered, successful individuals together, they are going to talk business.

The Clubhouse is not a place to make pitches and gain sales. It is however a place where the best will help the upcoming to succeed. Then you find your sales offsite are skyrocketing due to the networking and brand development done on the app. If you are a speaker, ask everyone in the room to follow you. Try to follow everyone in the room.

In Clubhouse you learn what people think and what the current trends are in investments, startups, and creative ideas.

Other Ways to Make Money

Successful online businesspeople usually identify multiple income streams to make their fortunes. This can be true for you as well on Clubhouse. There are many ways to monetize your time in the app. Here are some ways to make cash outside of your normal business field.

- Be a paid moderator.
- Get paid to write other's bios and profiles.
- Be a paid speaker.
- Be a paid Networker – help others build their network.
- Be a paid Clubhouse coach.
- Be a paid Room Notetaker.
- Be a paid Connector.
- Be a paid Club Manager

Other Thoughts

Here are just a few additional thoughts on building your brand and business on Clubhouse.

Entrepreneurs like John Perry and celebrities like Felicia Horowitz are holding events that you should attend. John Perry holds a Monday Morning Meeting for Entrepreneurs. You should be there. Even if you are not an entrepreneur, drop by and listen for a while. You gather plenty of ideas you can use in your own business.

Felicia Horowitz is the host of incredible dinner parties. There are thousands of users at her parties. Be there. Treat it like an in-person dinner party.

If you are comfortable socializing in larger groups, then just join one. Introduce yourself and listen until you have something to contribute. If you are more comfortable one-one, then find the person you want to talk to and open another room so you can have that conversation. When you are finished you can go back to the main party and begin to work the room again. Any marketer, salesperson or entrepreneur knows the value of this kind of socialization. Now you can do it from your living room in your sweats.

Most movers and shakers enjoy it this way. They can be multi-tasking while they are attending events on Clubhouse. When in person conferences can be held again, I do not think there will be as many as before COVID-19. There will be some but even at those you will find some participants with earbuds listening to Clubhouse while attending a session at the in-person conference.

This is because Clubhouse has shown us that personal and business success is based on authentic, deep, personal relationships.

Events build your pool of customers. Describe your event in a way that attracts potential customers. Yet do not make it an elevator sales pitch. You have 200 characters for your event description. Use them well. Use emojis in your event description as well. Make an emoji the first character in your event description then use another one about 100 characters later. Do not let your host or anyone else create your event. Clubhouse will know that you created the event and reward you.

Here's a good example from an anonymous Clubhouse user. He hosted several rooms and events that were engaging and provided interesting discussions. This user was a salesperson and by the time he closed his room, enough users had followed him to his off app to his website and made purchases that surpassed his monthly sales quota in one day.

Freebies that introduce listeners to your website and your products and services are a big part of your soon to be success. Of course, you cannot give out hats, cups, or even pens in this virtual environment. So, give away a class, a book, a gift certificate for your services. With these gifts you not only pique the interest of the listeners, but you also lead them right to your website to make their purchases.

Because listeners that enjoy the discussions in your rooms or the events you host will go to your profile for more information, make sure that profile sings. Make sure your followers know how to DM (direct message) you or get to your Twitter account.

If you have a lot of new people who come to your event, it might be fun to hold a welcome party for them and let them get acquainted with you and with the culture and rules of Clubhouse. You can do this in another Clubhouse room.

I do not recommend this, but some users have sold their invitations to those who have FOMO (fear of missing out). Invitations have sold from a few hundred dollars to over seventy-five hundred dollars.

Finally make sure you SEO (search engine optimization) your profile in the same way you would your website. Users will find you by searching these keywords. Then open as many rooms as you can for venture capitalists, entrepreneurs, and others who are looking for business opportunities and projects to support.

You can see how Clubhouse is an excellent platform for building your brand and marketing yourself. It is in this marketing of yourself that you will find you gathers many followers. I've had my team create "over the shoulder" type training videos for Clubhouse step-by-step to show you how I use it in your business.

In the next chapter we will look at the potential pitfalls of using the Clubhouse and how you might avoid them.

"Over the Shoulder"

STEP-BY-STEP

Training Videos

To get access visit:

ClubhouseTraining.APP

Chapter Ten:
Avoiding the Pitfalls while Leveraging Clubhouse

In Chapter nine, I discussed all the positive reasons why you should be on Clubhouse to enhance your business and build brand recognition. In this chapter I will review some of the pitfalls and potential slips you should avoid in order to be successful.

Pitfalls

To quickly review: Clubhouse is a fairly new audio-only drop in application. Rather than organize the platform by individual users, the Clubhouse is organized by rooms where conversations on specific content occur. This is still a Beta program that is entry by invitation only leading to a lot of MOFO enthusiasm

Clubhouse is a virtual conference with keynote speakers and a large crowd in one room and many smaller discussions in break out rooms. Then you might move on to a conference "cocktail party" where you can mix informally with other participants.

When you hear about Clubhouse from people who are not members you might think the site is messy and chaotic. Everyone talking and no one listening? Why is it invitation only? Is it a bunch of intellectual self-proclaimed elites? Why would a person spend hours on an app where they see nothing and just listen to conversations? It does not sound appealing when it is described in that manner does it?

The first and perhaps the biggest pitfall of the Clubhouse application is believing the negative talk and not seeking an invitation. Do not pay attention to the noise. Go and find out for yourself. There has much talk that Clubhouse is just a bunch of techies, venture capitalists and a few others. It was not a very diverse place according to this talk. Again, go find out for yourself.

Clubhouse might have started as a Silicon Valley exclusive club, but it not that anymore. In order to avoid this the Clubhouse administrators intentionally sought out and invited Black users in particular. This influx of new users led to an explosion of new conversations particularly around media and entertainment. Clubhouse began to evolve and still is. So, do not listen to the negative hype. If you can get an invitation take it and find out for yourself.

The one big problem with Clubhouse so far has been a lack of control by anyone over either the content or the language of the conversations. It does not seem at this time that the Clubhouse team is not able to prevent or even moderate hate speech, verbal abuse, or abusive subjects. The app has been criticized for allowing misinformation, antisemitism, and harassment.

Another potential pitfall is based on the fact that in Clubhouse there is no recording, transcript of any kind of record of the session. Once the room is closed it's really closed. Do not fall into the trap of trying to go around this rule by making your own transcript or recording. You can be suspended, or you can be kicked off the app if you are caught doing so.

If you want or need to use any of the conversation in any room for your blog or an article, then you must get permission from every person in the room to do so. Imagine how difficult that would be with people dropping in and dropping out all the time. It would be impossible.

Remember I mentioned in Chapter Nine that the only way to do this is to make it known in the title and description of the room that the conversation will be used in an article. Do not share others' intellectual property and do not incentivize others to share conversations that are not their own.

By the same token if you miss something in a room you missed it. It's not coming back around. This is why you might end up spending 6 or 7 hours at a time on the app. This could be at the expense of your business or your family. So, if you want the benefits of Clubhouse, schedule for the rooms you want to attend and plan to spend the whole day or night in that room. If the discussion is with venture capitalists discussing your project, you cannot leave. On the other hand, do not get so caught up in an interesting or entertaining discussion when you should be writing your blog.

The fact that this is an audio-only app is for the most part a good thing. As mentioned in previous chapters you can be on Clubhouse while you are making dinner or folding your laundry. However, you cannot multitask by watching a movie while on Clubhouse. I guess you could watch a sporting event at the same time as being on the Clubhouse, as long as you are not an overly enthusiastic and vocal fan.

Do not take at face value what other Clubhouse users say happened in a room you were not in. Because of the no record rule, there can be a lot of misinformation about what was said in the room. What was said could be taken out of context as well. Avoid quoting or sharing freely what others tell you about a room you were not in. We know without a transcript of official record you will get different perspectives from different people.

Although not against the rules, do not fall the habit of opening rooms that have a celebrity as the heart of the discussion without that celebrity being aware. For instance, you might want to have a room to discuss the career of Carol Burnett Everyone interested in Carol Burnett would flood to your room. Some unflattering things might be said about Carol Burnett.

Carol herself or friends of hers might drop in to hear what is being said. You do not want to be open to criticism for misinformation of false statements about a living celebrity. Now substitute a more contemporary celebrity like Jay Z or Oprah. The point is, it is easy to fill your room by raising a discussion about a celebrity, or a controversial topic.

If you are there to build your brand and market your skills, stay away from controversy. Do not take the easy route to acquiring a lot of followers. Packing a room with followers that have expressed no interest in why you are on the app will not benefit you in the long run. It's like copying a list of names and addresses from a contact list and calling it your leads. Will those leads turn into sales? Not very likely.

Do not confuse this potential pitfall with the example in the previous chapter about the man who collected enough leads in on room to make his monthly sales quota in a day. The room he was in had a direct connection to what he had to offer the listeners.

The worst-case scenario is if you have to report another user to the administrators because of inappropriate or abusive vocalizations or topics. You can do this anonymously and it is best to do it when you are still in the room.

If you are in the room when you report and incident, then the Clubhouse team can investigate it while there is still a recording of the conversation. This recording only exists for the purpose of investigating a complaint. It is destroyed as soon as the room closes. So, report the incident while you are in the room by going to the offending user's profile. Tap on the three dots in the top corner and you can then report the incident.

If you cannot file the incident while in the room, you can still do so later from your own profile. Tap on the same three dots and complete the incident report.

Just remember in this case there is no recording for the Clubhouse team to use for their investigation. They will still conduct an investigation, but your best evidence will be gone.

This concludes the shortest chapter in this book. Avoid the pitfalls and you will have an incredible experience on Clubhouse. This concludes the shortest chapter in this book. Avoid the pitfalls and you will have an incredible experience on Clubhouse. Yes, there are problems. Yes, there are trolls, scams, and questions about moderation and harassment. You can still avoid these issues and have a great time on Clubhouse.

Speaking of experiences, Chapter Eleven will focus on the real experiences of many Clubhouse users.

Chapter Eleven:
In Their Experience

In this chapter, I will share with you some of the experiences of individuals and small groups when interacting on Clubhouse. Though some of these tales may have been published elsewhere, I am not going to use anyone's real name. In order to respect their privacy all names will be alias.

Since coming online, Clubhouse has been both a big hit and at times a source of distress or abuse for a few. I am mostly interested in other's experiences using Clubhouse for business applications. However, I have already touched on some of the negative experiences people have had on Clubhouse. I won't rehash them here.

Some of the people who have recently been on Clubhouse are venture capitalist Marc Andreessen of Andreessen Horowitz, MC Hammer, Oprah, Jack Dorsey – a well know tech entrepreneur and philanthropist and rapist E-40. They have been joined by comedian/actor Hannibal Buress, and many well-known entrepreneurs in many different industries such as Grant Cardone, Daymond John, Lupe Fiasco and Tyrese Gibson.

What are they talking about? What has their experience been like? For all of the above celebrities, musicians, writers and businesspeople, the experience has been good enough to keep them coming back for more. There have been discussions about the future of rap music, about the recent Supreme Court decisions, the election and racism in America. Black Lives Matter has been a source of many conversations and of course there is much discussion about life during and after COVID-19.

The exciting thing about these experiences is that they have been shared by ordinary people from all over and every profession. There have been shows, debates, lectures, book clubs, and pitches for new products or services. All of these people come back repeatedly because the conversation is so stimulating and the business opportunities surprising. It is a place where deep connections are made, and friendships developed. We all know that old axiom that people do business with people they like.

Experience #1:

I am a 23-year-old woman with a degree in music and no idea what to do with my future. I came to Clubhouse at the invitation of a mentor from college. At first, I thought of it, as many do, like a podcast that was live. Then I thought it was more like Twitter because it centered on one person as a time. Leaders can talk passionately for hours on subjects they care about and the rest of us gain knowledge and value.

Then I realized it was none of the above. It was something new. It was something more exciting than any other social media site. It was a place where we could socialize in a different way, learn new things, and make new friendships. It was this because it was a place where people revealed themselves and spoke from the heart. Even if it was an entrepreneur talking about their product or service, it came from the heart.

It was not a sales pitch. In a session with a couple of well-known venture capitalists and several entrepreneurs, I finally got up the nerve to raise my hand. I was surprised when the moderator called on me and I moved to the stage. There I began to share my dream of opening an online business where young musicians could come and create with other young musicians. They could make tapes to send to producers or everyday people could make musical gifts for their friends and families.

I found myself in an intense discussion of this idea that others built on until the idea became a project that 3 or 4 of us were willing to take on. With all the support and advice from other entrepreneurs I felt confident enough to pursue my dream.

Experience #2:

I am an aspiring poet. I am also a young Black man. I was introduced to Clubhouse by some of my Black musician friends. At first, I wasn't sure of this audio-only app but since our passions of music and poetry were verbal, I thought I would give it a try. People seem to be coming back because it's a place where they can talk for hours at a time and leave each day feeling better rather than worse, because they have deepened friendships, built new ones, and learned something new. Clubhouse allows for conversations that are spontaneous, collaborative, and casual.

Because we were a group of young Black men in a room together, there were some passionate and angry discussions of the treatment of Black men in America. We ranted against the institutional racism that ruled our lives. Then one day we let a couple of white men in, and the conversation changed. They listened, really listened. They were not defensive. They were not condescending. They listened. My whole perspective was changed. Not that a couple of white men listening eliminates 400 years of racism. No that is not what happened. What happened is I changed. I changed because I did not believe white men could listen. The environment in Clubhouse made this happen.

Experience #3:

Reddit gave a lot of us an interesting experience as software-focused users and start up opportunists. The started a group of users in the field. They began with users of Hacker News then opened it up. It was early in the life of Clubhouse when this happened. We have been reaping the benefits ever since. Many of us migrate from Digg to Clubhouse to participate in these discussions.

Experience #4:

I'm just a casual user. I was not in it for business reason. However, I found Clubhouse to be a nice break from Tik Tok, Zoom and Team applications. It was more relaxing because I did not have to worry about what I was wearing or how I looked. I did not have to think about what my home or office might look like in the background. What keeps me coming back to Clubhouse is the variety of discussions and opportunities for learning. It is the real friendships and community you develop and deepen every time you meet with the same people. And yes, for casual users like me it is the chance to talk to Oprah or Jay Z that draws me in.

I know there are opportunities for business, brand building and marketing. I know there are entrepreneurs around every corner. This is not what draws me to Clubhouse, though it might be useful in the future.

Experience #5:

Unlike a lot of users on Clubhouse, I am not a spring chicken. I am 62 years old and have been in business for a while. I do OK but I am not in any way a super successful entrepreneur. So, when a friend invited me to Clubhouse, I was not sure it would be for me. However, I have found a couple of things that are really helpful to me in my small business.

First Clubhouse has allowed me to keep up with trends in the business community and in the society in general. If I just go to the right rooms where people in my industry are, I gain a lot of useful information. What is the next big thing in my industry? What are industry leaders talking about and what is my competition doing?

Secondly, I found that if I host a room that asks for feedback on my products or services, I usually got it. It was especially productive if I had a freebie to give everyone in the room. Usually, it would be a demonstration on YouTube that I gave away. That way if hundreds of users came to the session I would not run out of freebies. At the very least I could build my network of business associates and potential customers.

Experience #6:

Here we have a bright young entrepreneur in the fashion industry. Her goal was to have a six-figure business before she turned thirty. She met that goal and then began to mentor other young entrepreneurs. Soon she was sent an invitation to join Clubhouse.

I was not sure if there was any benefit for me to join this new social media platform. I do not have a lot of time for social media as it is. However, once I learned about the top-level connections being made on Clubhouse, I had to reconsider. This live voice only application seemed to be attracting some of the most prominent and sought-after business and industry leaders in the world.

I decided to accept the invitation. To my pleasant surprise, I found myself in conversations with many of the top businesspeople in the world. Speaking one on one with some of the most influential thinkers and entrepreneurs in the world opened up possibilities I had not considered. Within two days of joining the application, I had hundreds of followers. Many of the Clubhouse followers also followed me to Twitter and Instagram. From there they followed me to my website and other social media platforms. This is my experience and what I have learned so far from being on Clubhouse:

You can authentically interact with famous and prominent people from all over the world. The first room I visited when I joined was a "Business Growth" room. On the stage I quickly found the Shark Tank investors from the United States, Tiffany Haddish, and as others have mentioned Grant Cardone. They were on Clubhouse to offer their experience and to add value to your Clubhouse experience. I was a successful entrepreneur, but I was not in the same category with these guys.

Still, they allowed me to talk. They answered my questions. They gave advice on my projects in the making and seemed genuinely appreciative of my mentoring work. Since the only way to interreact with anyone on Clubhouse is through voice communication, you just have to be comfortable talking and sharing what you know. It's easier though because I do not have to worry about dressing up. Clubhouse listeners really want to hear what you have to say, or they would not be there.

If you do not know already, Clubhouse will help you to learn what the value is that you have to offer to others in this type of setting. You can then share your value with all your followers and potential followers. I'm comfortable asking to be recognized and invited to the stage to talk.

Even if you are not, the voice only platform makes it easier as no one will see you or know who you are by anything but your username. The more you are on stage the more followers you get. The more followers you have the more potential clients or sales you have. Let your followers know that they can DM you off of your Twitter or Instagram account. DMs are the best way to connect, to share your expertise or to build your brand.

I also learned that if you are going to do it, now is the time to do it. Get in before the application goes public. I know when here that an application is in its Beta stage, we expect a lot of glitches and updates. Do not get fooled by that way of thinking.

Clubhouse in Beta is probably better than it will be when it goes public. It is small enough now to have real, authentic, and intimate conversations. I worry that after the platform goes public, there won't be as "free" access to the top-level people that we have now. Rooms will be more crowd much of the time and your opportunity to speak will be less.

Experience #7:

I'm also a musician but it took me a little while to find Clubhouse or get interested in it. Once I was invited and found myself engaged in the application, I knew Clubhouse had exciting potential for musicians like me. I know Clubhouse has rules about not recording or transcribing what happens in a room without the consent of everyone in the room. So, because of I am just going to give you the highlights of what I noticed and what I can see down the road.

I think Clubhouse is and will be a great application for musicians of all stripes.

It seems that this audio-only concept has really taken off. Some of the biggest names in many industries are on the site including many musicians. At the present the musicians are just talking but soon they could be performing. Already there are many artists, actors, and investors on the site.

What if you are sitting on a new song and you happen to drop into a room where one of the biggest music producers in the world is holding court? Would you stay till almost the end of the conversations? Would you speak? Would you tell him about your song?

Just a small sampling of people on Clubhouse who have been of great interest to me includes: D-Nice, 21 Savage, MC Hammer, Jay Z, E-40, The Game, and Questlove. This is not just another platform. What is different here is the speed with which real time conversations take place and the intimate authenticity of the voice. You know how hard it is to judge the feelings and meanings of text messages at time. Text without voice is often hard to decipher. On the other hand, voice without video is much clearer. Besides, we are not all comfortable in the video/voice world of Zoom.

Clubhouse works especially well for musicians. One of the biggest advantages of the Clubhouse for musicians is the access to connections and networks that we would not usually have access to. Being in the same room with the movers and shakers of the music industry along with famous musicians and artists is rare.

Not only is this possible in the Clubhouse but you know you are talking to the right person by hearing their voice. If you need a manager, a producer, a marketer, or a photographer/videographer you can get hooked up on Clubhouse. Another terrific opportunity for musicians on Clubhouse is the exposure you can get for your music.

Open a room and host an open mic for yourself and your friends. Invite all your followers to join you. You might consider getting an emcee for the room, so you are free to share your music. You could have a war of the bands and invite music industry people that you follow. I participated in some of these myself.

Here are some rooms where music was the focus. "Why Musicians Need Managers.," "Networking for Musicians," "Mixing and Mastering Your Songs." In other rooms there will be professionals and artists that are more than willing to share their expertise and answer your questions.

Many artists were willing to share their stories and explain how they were not an "overnight success." Almost everyone sharing their story had worked for years to make it.

While you are struggling to make it, it can get pretty lonely out there. However, with Clubhouse you can find your community of likeminded people and musicians. If you cannot find your community here, you can make it. The best place to find them is in the clubs. Unfortunately, Clubhouse does not yet have a search feature for finding specific clubs, but they are working on it. There also might be a paid membership sometime down the road.

By far the part the aspect of Clubhouse I enjoyed the most and I think has the most potential for musicians is the actual performance. While on Clubhouse I learned that there was a complete audio version of the Lion King being performed. A virtual cast of 40 joined by a choir, band and narrators was spread out across twenty cities.

Since there was no lag time, it was a major success and leads the way for many more creative performances of all kinds. It would be great to host a jam session with a lot of other musicians that anyone can drop in on it at any time. If they can do a full-scale Broadway musical, I can host a jam session.

You will want to host your room in the "Music Mode" and be connected to a program like iRg. This will improve the sound quality for performances.

In Their Own Words

The following are actual quotes, and the speaker is identified.

"This app (Clubhouse) is like if "Houseparty" was audio, and it was about people's interests instead of your friend groups. It makes (it) easy to go into a conversation ...it does not feel like the same kind of pressure as video chats. It's made better for introverts than other apps I've seen."

- Ben Parr, Cofounder Octane AI.

"I check into Clubhouse more than 15 to 20 times a day to see what's going on. I do not do this with Facebook. I think it's up there right now as one of the apps I use most frequently. I'm there to learn and listen, and it gives me a good enough reason to be on the product. Like, 'Hey, I can learn something here today.'"

-Sriram Krishnan- investor and venture capitalist

"It's (Clubhouse) clearly happened so fast because of where we are now because people crave places and opportunities to meet new people. But I do not think it will go away when the crisis (pandemic) is over. People are going to make more cautious decisions about whether it's worth to go meet people in person or not. People will go step by step. They're not going to go from zero to 10 hours when hanging out with friends. This pattern of online habits won't go away."

- **Masha Drokova – Founder Day One Ventures**

These are the real-life experiences of a handful of people in Clubhouse. For the most part these experiences have been positive. There have been times when a conversation turns to passionate negativity, name calling and abuse of some listeners and speakers. This is the exception not the rule. Yet it is something that Clubhouse will have to correct with rules, moderation, and enforcement actions.

So, if you want success on Clubhouse like several of these people have had, it just takes a few consistent steps to get there. Once you are in, be sure to invite others as you can. Open rooms with topics related to your business. Invite everyone you follow and everyone who follows you.

Title the room in a way that will be enticing to the largest group – a group that should include venture capitalists. You want as many venture capitalists and entrepreneurs as possible. Having these folks present lends itself to exciting conversations, opportunities to gain support for new projects and a way to increase your business contacts.

As you talk about your projects and products you will get immediate and valuable feedback. You might get an investment offer, or you might get useful information on improving your business. In this room or other rooms share what it is about your business that you are passionate about. Why are you passionate about this and who does it help? What problems does it solve? The more you can share this the more followers you will gain.

"Over the Shoulder"

STEP-BY-STEP

Training Videos

To get access visit:

ClubhouseTraining.APP

Chapter Twelve:
Case Studies

In this chapter I will review some case studies of those who are currently or have participated in Clubhouse. Again, confidentiality is important and the members in the cases will remain confidential. This is the longest chapter in this book and it just might be the most important one.

Case Study #1

User A is a high-level real estate investor, and he began to drop in on rooms where his industry and interests were being discussed. He was immediately captivated by the users in the room and the discussion going on. It did not take long for to make connections with others like him. User B was also a high-level real estate investor with a podcast and influencer group.

Soon User and User B were hosting several rooms on business, entrepreneurship, and investment real estate. Together these two entrepreneurs have hosted various live watch parties and have hosted up to one thousand users at a time. Together they have helped many upcoming entrepreneurs and listened to many ideas for new projects.

Together they have helped get several new projects off the ground and held discussions that came up with new and innovative ideas.

Case Study #2

User C is a life coach, a business coach, and a marketer. She came onto Clubhouse early in its Beta form. User C's motivation in accepting the Clubhouse invitation was to help others get started or flourish in the industries she flourished in. She also believed that acquiring many followers would be a boost to her own business.

User C felt that a lot the early members of Clubhouse were marketers and into content discussions. She found this environment to be exciting and worth her time. For her Clubhouse is analogous to that conference I referenced earlier. People who love to network at conferences would love Clubhouse as well. It was clearly the right social media for a pandemic. User C saw her followers grow by the hundreds and her new clients coming from these followers. For User C, Clubhouse was a lifesaver during this pandemic.

Case Study #3

User D is an entrepreneur and investor. He joined Clubhouse early, believing that being first was really important. Not knowing where Clubhouse would go, he understood what it was now. What it was now could be a goldmine to entrepreneurs and investors everywhere.

Many users can develop a large number of followers but unless you were the first and the best in your field, your success would be limited. User D saw how powerful this position on Clubhouse would be once the application went public. Now is the time to build your brand recognition and market your skills and knowledge. In this way User D attracted followers who were not just interested in what he had to share, but ready to use his services outside the Clubhouse.

One of User D's ways to do this is to hold regularly scheduled discussions on a variety of topics that would be of interest to the same type of user. He also understood that offering a free digital gift to every participant in every discussion. He was also successful in getting the users in his rooms to ping their networks and those networks would ping theirs and they would be able to multiply networks very quickly,

Case Study #4

User E is a well-known entrepreneur with a television show, and he does several television commercials. He is now an investor and spends most of his time help others to bring exciting and different products to market. He has been known to host rooms that can last for hours where aspiring entrepreneurs present their product or service to User E and other venture capitalists in the room. Several times a few of the entrepreneurs made deals with either User E or the other venture capitalist. User E believes this is a great way to get new products on the market and for him to make good investment choices. He says he sees more new ideas and products on Clubhouse than he does anywhere else. User E believes every aspiring entrepreneur and every venture capitalist should get on board before the app goes public.

Case Study #5

User F is in the retail business and in this pandemic, he has seen a marked decline in his business including online sales. He had already decided that he needed a new way to attract customers when he received his invitation to Clubhouse. He quickly scooped up the invite and jumped in. User F was planning to gather a group of followers and bringing them back to his retail online store and his retail application. User F was a big believer in apps for smart phones in this pandemic.

However, User F found Clubhouse to be just as engaging and creative as an app of his own. As he began to drop in and out of rooms, he always attempted to be a speaker and share his insights. The goal was still to gather as many followers as possible. He just didn't expect to get hundreds in two days and at least fifty DMs.

Once he saw what Clubhouse could do, User F began to host his own rooms with contests and giveaways to attract even more followers. His total sales increased by 5% with the followers from Clubhouse being more than 50% of those sales. The buyers from Clubhouse also spent more money and bought more items than customers gleaned from other sites or in the retail stores.

User F also saw that these Clubhouse followers were loyal customers, returning several times within the year. He decided to up the ante and added a Club to his repertoire on the app. User F created fashion shows, designer discussions and brought in famous designers. He believes the best is yet to come and unlike many of the entrepreneurs on Clubhouse, he is not wary of the app going public. He just thinks it will afford more opportunities for sales for someone like him.

Case Study # 6

User G is a business owner and an entrepreneur. He belongs to a lot of social media sites and "clubs." However, he describes himself as "obsessed" with Clubhouse. Many of the conversations he listens to on the app are ones he would otherwise have to pay to hear. He gains more insights and marketing tidbits than any of his other "clubs" give him.

User G also define Clubhouse as a community where "the opportunity to network and collab is endless." After only a week on the app, this user had almost 1000 followers. He compared it to the months it took to get even a few hundred followers on Instagram.

Now he starts rooms and hosts events to bring in even more followers. He gets endless requests from other users to work with him.

User G also reports that he has seen many other users land clients from the followers who DM them. One bit of advice from User F is to be sure you connect your Twitter and Instagram accounts so you can be followed off the Clubhouse application to where you can actually do business.

Case Study #7

User G has a lot of feedback for others coming on the application. She really feels it is great for business, marketing, and coaches. She was a little shy at first in rooms where so many successful people gathered. It took her awhile to become a speaker and in turn to gather many followers. Once she got started though, there was no stopping her.

User G is an entrepreneur and a life coach. She was surprised by all the business-related rooms on Clubhouse but also saw that she could profit from being in rooms with topics like spirituality, life changes, starting over.

As a coach she had a lot to offer in these rooms and soon followers began to pile up. She gained thousands of followers and hundreds of DMs in just one month on the application. She also began to gain new clients off the site. As she spoke about her life coaching experiences, more and more Clubhouse users wanted to know more.

Now when User G hosts a room or raises her hand to speak, she introduces herself and has a one sentence tag line that tells everyone in the room what she does. She also invites her entire network to any room, Club, or event she is involved in. Her clientele has increased to the point where she will be hiring another life coach to join her.

Case Study #8

User H is an author. When he received his invitation to join the Clubhouse application he was bemused and intrigued. He wondered why he would be invited to such an app, but he downloaded it anyway. Now he was really confused by the blank screen he saw in front of him. What was this? Was it a joke his friends were playing on him? Just as he was thinking this the screen came to life and another Clubhouse user welcomed him. This user took all the time User H needed to tour the application and learn how to use it.

As a writer, User H was definitely interested in what the app might have to offer. At the same time his tour guide informed him that everyone on Clubhouse had been informed of his arrival. Some of his readers and fans followed him immediately. In his own words, User H described Clubhouse as "working because it is somewhere between a podcast and a party, and people love both of those things." He also found many new ideas and topics to write about in the future,

Case Study #9

User J is a general retailor that though he found same success on the application, he also found some things that frustrated him. What was exciting for so many was frustrating for User J. The fact that there was no record of the conversation in the room frustrated him as he felt he was missing out on so much valuable information and discussion. He could not be there 24 hours a day and wished he could get a transcript from a certain room's discussion. This was particularly true when there was more than one room going on at the time that he wanted to attend.

His second frustration came from the discussion in the room itself. Even with a moderator the conversations do not stay on topic. This is another aspect that many people like about Clubhouse that frustrated User J. There is also the phenomenon of new people entering the room all the time and unless your moderator is very good at resetting the room, they will ask questions that were answered hours ago. Thus, there is less new content because you have to repeat what has already been discussed.

For User J there is the fear that if Clubhouse does not "make it" one could lose all the followers and time invested in it. The key to overcoming this fear is to make sure your followers join you in your Twitter and Instagram accounts. Then you can move them over to your own websites so your effort in Clubhouse is not futile.

Finally, though User J has stayed on the app and collected many followers he also worries about what will happen when the app goes public. Can you have a room with 10,000 people in it and still have the intimate discussions you can have now? Will Clubhouse have to move to a paid membership that guarantees smaller discussion groups? Will the movers and shakers of industry, music, art, and entertainment stay with the platform once it goes public?

Case Study #10

User K is again a retailer but of her interior design services. Her experience of the Clubhouse has been overwhelmingly positive. She began by speaking in rooms she had entered as a listener. She also spoke up in a business centered room and had much the same experience as our other case studies. Within days she had 60 followers and her Instagram account garnered an additional 100 followers.

Once in a room full of entrepreneurs and investors, User K raised her hand and asked for advice on jumpstarting their business. In doing so the user had to explain what her business was. Within an hour of that room closing members of the audience, speakers and moderators went to her profile and linked to her Instagram account. From there they followed her to her website and ordered services and/or products.

She was amazed and rushed back to Clubhouse to set up her own rooms and discuss interior design. In so doing,

User K could both offer advice, expertise and knowledge to other start-ups or struggling businesses and still grow her own.

Case Study #12 – J Franco – Branding, Marketing and Social Media

Deviating from the anonymous users because J Franco has written articles on her experience with Clubhouse. (links can be found in the references) She found it to be "a Godsend" in this pandemic for all of us who want to be networking and socializing for business reasons. It is the same for everyone who is missing their business conferences or annual meetings. It is a place to garner knowledge from others in one's field.

J shares that she was in a room with John Lee, CEO, and a writer for Forbes. There was a wealth of business information and ideas in that one room. Her experience on Clubhouse leads her to believe it will grow exponentially in the next few years. J Franco sees voice as a "primary social media trend in 2021", and beyond, transforming social media as we know it today.

Case Study #13 - Adam Lashinsky

This case study is based on several articles that Adam has written. (links can be found in the references) Adam admits to being dragged kicking and screaming into the Clubhouse application. Like our author in Case Study #8, he was skeptical but also intrigued.

Adam compares his first experience with Clubhouse to his first experience with understanding the real use for Twitter. While traveling with another entrepreneur and blogger, he was told that his companion posted a link on Twitter every time he posted an article in his blog. This allowed his thousands of Twitter followers to see the link and follow it to his blog.

A light bulb went off for Adam as he realized that bloggers who had advertisers paying them by the number of readers could create a goldmine this way. For the first time he appreciated the business applications of Twitter. The same was true for the Clubhouse. Sure, he had heard of it. Many of his friends and collogues were getting invited and logging on. Adam was skeptical as usual and turned down a few chances to get an invitation.

Eventually he relented and found Clubhouse to be the same kind of exciting place for indirect revenue generation as he found Twitter to be. Clubhouse was not just a hangout for techies and celebrities from Silicon Valley. No, Adam discovered just how important this application can be to building a brand, marketing knowledge, developing followers and making a profit.

This application was endless in its ability to have multiple conversations simultaneously about multiple topics. It's similar to an old-fashioned AM radio talk show before we all abandoned radio for the internet. Like the talk show, the moderator keeps the discussion in line and cuts off the speakers who are irrelevant or irreverent. The host might bring in a guest or a panel, but the discussion is open to anyone who can get in.

The difference is these radio talk shows were not airing around the clock, seven days a week. Clubhouse is always there, and, in this pandemic, it is more appreciated than it might be at another time in history. Adam was sold in a hurry, seeing all the possibilities for the app. Unlike the one subject talk show, Clubhouse let Adam move from one conversation to another at will. If he felt he had enough of one talk, he could leave and enter another room. Soon Clubhouse was taking up an awful lot of Adam's time.

In just a few days' time Adam listened in to talks on the art of persuasion with Guy Kawasaki, the stock market upheaval around GameStop shares, and a pitch for Ricki Lake's "The Business of Birth Control" documentary. Then he sat in on talks designed to help up and coming entrepreneurs.

Adam was then able to sit in on a "town hall" with the CEO of Alpha Exploration that owns the Clubhouse application. These meetings with the founders and officers are held weekly and any topic is on the table. Davison peeked Adam's interest with a conversation about how to make money from the application. The intent is to develop an Android version and to go public soon.

Davison also spoke to the future of Clubhouse saying he didn't expect to earn money from advertising but perhaps they would let users charge for talks, classes or coaching and earn a percentage from that. There was also talk of a paid premium type membership.

This conversation did bring some doubt into Adam's mind about Clubhouse. Will it lose its momentum when the pandemic ends and we go back to live face to face interactions? Will it be overwhelmed when it goes public? Will it lose its excitement when it is no longer an exclusive, invitation only club? With these questions Adam is still skeptical despite seeing the impressive benefits to small businesses and entrepreneurs Clubhouse offers. Already there is controversy on the app in terms of racism, sexism, anti-Semitism and more. The Clubhouse team has tried to answer these controversies with rules on acceptable and unacceptable behavior that could get you expelled from the app.

Whatever the future might be, Clubhouse has shown Adam that we are not all hooked on only communicating through texts, emails, and postings on Facebook. There is room in the business community and in the social communities for voice only application. Adam now believes that other internet sites and companies may soon follow the Clubhouse lead.

Case Study #14 – Steve James, Blogger

Steve's expedition into the world of Clubhouse was as eye opening as many of our other case study players. He thought perhaps this was just another social media application attempting to take a small share of the market from Facebook, Twitter, and Instagram.
Steve quickly found out that it was not a copycat, but rather a whole new type of social media. It is the first of its kind but Steve's experience with the application tells him

it won't be the last. Still, you have to wonder, what is so fascinating in listening to other people talk?

For one Steve found the audio-only format to be refreshing. No ranting posts or angry tweets. No misunderstood emails. Here you can hear the voice of the speaker and know the emotions they are feeling. Here you can have a conversation not a written back and forth shouting match. Here you can learn from the best in their fields and ask them to elaborate on things you do not quite understand. Steve found that Clubhouse was dynamic, exciting, informative, and perhaps even profitable.

It's conversations about things people care about, that are important to them. Unlike the beginnings of sites like Instagram or Pinterest, folks on Clubhouse are not posting verbal pictures of their most recent meal. Instead, they are meeting with a renowned chef to discuss the best of their recipes and how they can improve them. The chef might refer them to his live cooking classes on YouTube.

For Steve there was a real benefit in not having to think about how to word a post or a Tweet. It was refreshing to just talk about things, to just say what he wanted to say. You do not have to worry about the quality of the picture you want to post. You can just describe what you see in words or make the point you want to make. There is something elemental and essential about just using your voice – just YOUR voice.

Case Study #15 – Renee Halfway - "Young Success"

Renee Halfway is a student studying for her master's degree and a vision she calls Young Success. Renee is 21 years old and is all about helping other young women to find their dreams and make them real. Renee was introduced to Clubhouse not long ago but has already laid out for herself how it can help her business.

If you have a service business or an online business, Renee has found that Clubhouse is especially good for growing these. Yet is can be used to grow any type of business.

Renee hosts a room with weekly discussions and that featured four other women. The topics were anything to do with business and the other women were from various business fields. There was Brenna, an academic coach, Lauren, a business strategist, Mkenna, a social media manager and a Pinterest expert in Isabelle. Renne found that her business acumen was increased at every meeting and she always came away with something she could use of try.

The Renee dropped in a room the conversation was real estate and the speakers were three New York realtors. The discussion was educational and exciting. Renee learned about renting versus buying and what to look for in each case. Renee messaged them after the room was closed and learned that they were considering building a brokerage together. They had all generated a pile of leads from their sharing on Clubhouse.

Renee learned a few other things as well about Clubhouse. It is important to always bring value to whatever room you are in and whatever role you are in. If you are a listener in the audience then try to raise a question or point that is interesting. If you are a speaker always try to add information that will benefit the room.

When you are hosting a room or event keep it within your niche or business interest in some way. Renee has gone from beginner status to hosting or moderating rooms as often as possible. She even belongs to Female Clubhouse Entrepreneurs and is learning a lot while enjoying the women in the club.

Case Study # 16 - @stringstory

@Stringstory shared her experiences and thoughts about Clubhouse after less than a month on the app. @Stringstory is not coming to Clubhouse in the same way as most of the users I have discussed and shared with you. @Stringstory has the goal of building, leveraging and growing a community that is trusted and safe for business leaders and professionals.

After less than a month on the site @Stringstory is doing the work needed to get her own Club which she will call "The Trusted Voice." She quickly learned that Clubhouse was a "great way to find your voice and kickstart your personal brand." She found that unlike other social media sites with the Clubhouse voice only application other users really saw you. They heard in your voice what you believed in and stood for. They got a sense of your personality and your business smarts. You were in @Stringstory's words "a walking brand." Everything you say and the rooms you choose to go in speak of your brand.

Since you cannot hide it, use it. Be intentional about everything you say on Clubhouse and who you say it to. Make sure your bio says who you are in the way you want it to and includes links to your Instagram and Twitter accounts. Now make sure your profiles on all other sites match your profile on Clubhouse because people are going to follow you off the app.

One of the most important applications you can have off the Clubhouse site is LinkedIn. Though it may not be as exciting as it was in the beginning, LinkedIn is still a place where small businesspeople go to connect with others like them. Make sure your LinkedIn profile matches your Clubhouse profile. Maje sure your LinkedIn location is in your Clubhouse profile, even though it cannot be an active link at this time.

According to @stringstory she uses Clubhouse to build a community and a network that will follow her off the Clubhouse app. This is a way to build your brand, develop your business and get sales or clients. The more time you spend on Clubhouse, the better you will know your customers or clients.

Case Study # 17 – Gary Henderson

In the first twenty-four hours that Gary Henderson was on Clubhouse he amassed over two thousand followers on

Instagram and gained over ten Twitter followers. He also scheduled several strategy sessions and added an event the features a podcaster with more than 2.7 million followers worldwide.

Amazing? Not if you know what you are doing and what your goals are as Gary did. Already seen as a leader in his field Gary built on that reputation to increase his influence and followers. Even being at the top of his field, he still found people to talk to on Clubhouse that he would not normally run into in his offline activities.

Gary wanted to know if there was anything coming up or going on in his industry that he did not know about. So, he made the rounds, dropping in and out of several business conversations. Here are some tips that Gary learned to pass on to others joining Clubhouse. Gary recommends using your own name or your business name as your username. Some users chose the name of their blog and their username. Some business niches used keywords for their username that said who they were. Gary noted "Fitness Coach or Parenting Expert" were used.

Needless to say, Gary has found the Clubhouse application to be interesting and profitable.

Additional User Cases for Business

Here are just a few more examples of user cases specifically for business. All of the experiences in Chapter Eleven and cases in Chapter 12 involve business scenarios or businesspeople. But here are a few more in-depth examples of what you can do with Clubhouse.

Collaborate

Clubhouse is the perfect place to meet people who share your vision and your goals. You will also meet people who share your curiosity and imagination. You and your company might find that you want to collaborate with some of these people on future projects.

If you have a company with employees, invite them onto Clubhouse as well. They can learn from the people you want to collaborate with, and they can show off the value of your company. Teams within your company might collaborate with other teams in your company or they may find others to collaborate with as a team.

Network

For over twenty years now, networking has been a catchphrase in every industry in any part of the world. Network at conferences and network at the Chamber of Commerce After Hours is a requirement of a successful business. Network to find a career placement, network to change careers, network to start a business or to grow one.

Clubhouse gives you one more way to network on a very personal level. You are spending time with like-minded people and building a network. This network has people in your industry and people from many other industries. It might include your clients, your vendors, your investors.

It may seem that social media has made networking easier with texts, Tweets, and emails. To a certain extent this is true, however an audio-only site can bring a more human experience to all. Especially in this time of pandemic, but also when we begin to move out into the world again, these networks will be vital to your business.

Establish your Authority and Credibility

If you have been in business for more than a week you know that your name and your credibility are your business. Potential customers and clients need to know you word is good, you are an expert in your industry, and they can trust you. The most successful business relationships are built on this trust.

The first thing you want to achieve after joining Clubhouse is establishing that authority and credibility in your field. Get together with others in your field and host a room around the topic of your industry. Freely share your knowledge and expertise. Do not hold back. Be generous with your time and your expertise. It will come back to you many times over.

Build a Community

People do business with people they like. Your customers and clients want to know that they are important to you. You know who they are, and you know what is important to them. This is why the opportunity to build community in Clubhouse is so exciting to entrepreneurs, businesspeople, and venture capitalists. Personal communication with customers and clients will only enhance those relationships. So, build a community around your business and bring your customers into the family. They will be loyal to you and your company if you do.

Host a Virtual Event

Yes, you can host a virtual event on Zoom, a Webinar on Cisco, or a teleconference using your own systems. It is good to hold visual virtual events, but they can be very stressful and require elaborate planning and materials. The pandemic has shown us how valuable these virtual events can be even when we can travel and meet face to face again.

An audio-only virtual event may take a lot of the stress out of planning and organizing. You may be able to recruit the top experts in your field and some of the best thinkers in the world to you Clubhouse event. They do not have to prepare visuals for their presentation. They do not have to be sitting in an office. They do not even have to get dressed if they do not want to.

Hosting virtual events on Clubhouse will be one of your best endeavors on the app. You will fill the room with interested people – potential clients or customers. You can add everyone in the room to your network and ask them all to follow you. A virtual event on Clubhouse will generate excitement and interest. It will also get you noticed by the Clubhouse staff to open your own Club if you like.

This completes the case studies in this book, but there are thousands of more you could hear from and learn from. Getting on Clubhouse and starting the journey is your first step toward success.

In the next chapter, I will review all the most important things I have discussed so far.

Chapter Thirteen:
Conclusion – Is Clubhouse Right for You?

This book is designed to educate and excite you about the new audio-only social media application called Clubhouse. As every good educator knows, the best way to teach is to tell your audience what your presentation is about. We do this in the introduction. Then we tell you what we want you to know in the body of the book. Finally, we come to this chapter where I will tell you again in this conclusion what is I covered in body of the book.

So, to review:

What is Clubhouse and why should you care? In the early chapters of this book, I covered just exactly what this new application is and what it can do for you. After this detail view of the Clubhouse application, I looked at what it can do for your business and that are the potential pits fall?

The last three chapters have been focused on the real-life experiences of real people who use Clubhouse. Even though most of the users were kept confidential by the rules of the application, these users relayed their experiences.

They offered their insights and recommendations for how to make the best use of Clubhouse for building your brand and marketing yourself.

Here we go, Clubhouse is an audio, social media application. There is no visual, no texting, no typing and almost no emojis. Clubhouse is unique. It is also invitation only. You must be invited to join and there are only two ways to get invited. A current user must invite you, or you must request an invitation from Clubhouse.

Clubhouse is not just another social media site that happens to be audio. There are many exciting possibilities for business and marketing lurking within this application. To use Clubhouse to increase your brand recognition and customer base is a primary goal.

Here is a brief review of the description of Clubhouse. It is a real-time, online, audio-only social media application. You can talk with anyone in any open room, and you can talk about anything you want. It's a hands-free application that doesn't tie you to a screen or keyboard. You can cook, do laundry, ride a bike, or take a walk while being connected through Clubhouse to some of the most interesting people in the world.

Clubhouse is an iPhone only application. Android users will have to wait for their application to be developed. Right now, there are celebrities, top notch techies, entrepreneurs, capitol investors and "just ordinary folks." Clubhouse is now in a Beta stage. What will it look like when it is open to the public? Will all these high-end users still be there.

Right now, there is plenty of space for new users if you can get invited. The first thing to do is download the app from the Apple store. Then you can reserve Clubhouse to invite you. If you have friends on the app, they can invite you. Getting an invitation from someone in the Clubhouse already is easier than getting it from the administrator. This is true even though users do not have unlimited number of invitations to give out. Only about 10-12 invitations go out every day to the hundreds who are reserving their username.

Once you are in, you get one invitation to give to someone else. If that person joins you then get three more. You can also earn them as you interact on the site. Remember there is a back door. When you register your username anyone in your contacts who is already in the Clubhouse will be notified and they can let you in without using their invitation.

As I have said many times throughout this book, Clubhouse is populated by the best of the best in almost every field. Celebrities, artists, CEOs, CFOs, musicians, techies, and entrepreneurs. Just to remind you of a few members, Oprah might drop into any room. Ashton Kutcher, Chris Rock, Drake, MC Hammer, Kevin Hart or Jay Z might also drop in anywhere at any time.

Other conversations that have occurred in the Clubhouse include:

- MC Hammer's discussion of rap's history and future. You might also find MC discussing the impact of Covid 19 on prison populations. This discussion also included Shaka Senghor, Van Jone, Ben Horowitz, Marc Andreessen, and venture capitalists.

- In another room, you will find Ben Horowitz again, along with Hip hoppers and rappers. Fab 5 Freddy was there along with Jared Leto and Kevin Hart. Horowitz hopes to recruit new talent to bring to the Clubhouse.
- There are many technical discussions with current and past employees of Google, Microsoft, and others. There have been very serious discussions such as the "realities of being a Black man in America today."
- There is a group of the first hundred or so users that meets every night and stay up talking till 4 in the morning. They talk about anything but tech.
- You might find Kanye West, Estelle, Meek Mill or Tiffany Haddish in deep discussion with entrepreneurs from Silicon Valley in another room.

Let's remember what happens when you accept the invitation and download the application. What do you expect? You do not really know what to expect. The biggest surprise is those few moments when you open the app and see a blank screen. What a relief when that Clubhouse member appeared to show you the way.
Here is a quick review of the application as you enter the Hallway.

From the Hallway you can enter a room as a listener and member of the audience. There is a menu on top and rooms on the bottom. The top menu tells you the events that are scheduled, a Search command to find other members and the notifications. In the calendar you can share events through your contacts and links. You can also send the events to any other calendar you use. Last but not least you can add your own events to the calendar.

What to do first? Enter a room and listen. Start thinking how this application can help build your brand and your business. Remember to spend time with people who are passionate about the same things you are. Learn something from every room you enter and give value when you can.
Next follow everyone in every room you enter and invite them to follow you. Remember this is the biggest benefit to your business and your brand. Get others to know who you are.

Your Profile

Let me remind you again and again and again. Your profile is the most important thing you will do when you join Clubhouse. Again remember to set up a username that makes sense in respect to what you do and what you want to share. This is so important because you can change everything in your profile whenever you want *except* your username. That can only be changed once. Your profile needs to tell your story and do it in an easy to find, easy to absorb few sentences. You know that there are certain things that every profile has. Yet every profile is different, and you need to take your time and be as creative as you can when developing it.

As discussed in all the chapters starting with chapter four, the importance of your profile and taking care in creating it cannot be overstated.

Remember you need

- A picture which you can change anytime you like.
- Full name followed by your username.
- Number of people you are following.
- Number of people following you.
- Profile information that you can edit at any time. This is the important part and the part that requires your creativity. I've said it before. This is the section of your profile that will create interest and get people to follow you. This is also how your followers will get to your Instagram, Twitter, and website. Remember that you want to get the most important information in the first three sentences and make sure this is search engine optimized (SEO). You have 125 characters in those first three sentences so be concise and use any Twitter skills you have. Remember you cannot use live links.

Think about the dog trainer I discussed in the early chapters. What should her profile look like in order to get a lot of attention and a lot of followers? Here is a possible profile for this user.

- The first thing she will add is an emoji from the Clubhouse lists and that represents her business.
- She will have a picture of herself with her dogs. She might have a picture of her company if she has a

building that she can switch out with the self-portrait.

- Her Name – Julie Tomas 's Dog Training
- @Julie
- Her username - Julie's Dog Training
- Following 300 users
- Followed by 652 users
- Use another emoji to start this section. Remember you can write this section off the application and use any emojis or images you want. Then you can cut and paste it back into your profile.

- I am an enthusiastic dog lover. No bad dogs just untrained ones. Let me teach you to teach your dogs. + 17 years' experience + National Champion Obedience + Therapy Dogs (add in some dog emojis and happy people)
- Connect with me on my other sites:
- @Julie'sDog Training. Twitter/IG/YouTube --- Julie's Dog Training on FB + LinkedIn + www.Julie's Dog Training.com
- Let me help you help your dog! Basic obedience through Canine Good Citizen Training
- Love travel
- Entrepreneur
- Small business
- Animal Rescues and Abuse Prevention
- AKC Dog Breed expertise

Joined October 1, 2020

Member of (icons of clubs Julie belongs to)

Now let's take a look at my real profile. My profile is @Andybroadaway.

- The first thing you will see is my picture.
- This is followed by my name Andy Broadaway
- @andybroadaway
- Next, I have xxx followers and I am following xx
- Next, I have a money bag icon and Strategic Business Coach/Advisor. This is the most important thing I want people to know aout me. But remember you have the first three lines to get in the most important information.
- Next, I have a books icon and #1 Best-Selling Author/Speaker
- A PC icon and Content Publishing Strategist

Now I have competed the most important part of the profile because this is the snapshot that someone will receive when they click on my profile. If they want more information, you can provide as much as you want below these initial three lines. Here is the rest of my profile.

- Star icon and Clients hire me to help them impact more people and make more money.
- Bank Icon and Over the past 10 years, I have helped my private clients generate over 4.3 million $$$
- Mic Icon and I create brands off & online for speakers/authors/entrepreneurs
- Family icon and Proud father of six amazing children
- Icon and 28 years serial entrepreneur
- Icon and founded 9 business

Services Offered

- Strategic Business Strategy
- Successful Funnel System
- Event Production
- Book Publishing

Book Icon FREE Books:

www.2021yourbestyear.com

www.pivotbusinessbook.com

Location: Enterprise, NV

Why am I on GH? Networking, Team Building

Connecting with Experts & contribution

Follow me:

www.AndyBroadaway.com

IG @andybroadaway

Linkedin: www.linkedin.com/in/andybroadaway

Facebook: fb.com/TheAndyBroadaway/

Cash app: $andybroadaway

Book Icon Book Publishing Services

www.AbundantPress.com

@ andybroadaway

Joined Dec. 24, 2020

Nominated by TAMARA THOMPSON

These are just a couple of samples of the kind of information you need in your profile. Julie stresses her experience, authority in her field and the fact that she had trained dogs that were National Obedience Champions and others that were Therapy Dogs. If you are into animals especially dogs, you will want to follow her. Try to make your profile as interesting and self-explanatory as this one. Remember to link your profile to Instagram and Twitter.

Since I am a business consultant, I stress that background and how I help speakers and publish books. I have several ways that a user could follow me. You will note that I listed Instagram (IG) but not Twitter. I don't use Twitter for business at this time.

Now tap the gear icon and choose your settings. This is easy but again remember what is designed to do. Notifications regarding topics you are interested in allows you to choose topics. Information and Links, allows you to check any updates in the application, contact the Help Center, Report an Incident, Check the Community Guidelines, Terms of Service, and Privacy Policy. This is also where you will link to your Twitter and Instagram accounts.

Actions from the Hallway

Here is a quick reminder of what you can do from the Hallway besides enter a room.

- See how many invitations you have and send them to friends or colleagues.
- Search for other members using their username or key words. You would find our dog training under the key words' dogs, dog training, animals, travel and more.
- Check the calendar for events and upcoming room topics.
- Edit your profile – change your picture frequently.

Rooms

Once you enter a room from the hallway stay muted and remember you have to both raise your hand with the hand icon and be acknowledged and moved to the stage by a moderator. Remember there are only a few things you can do once you enter a room. They include muting and unmuting your microphone, raising your hand, Pinging others, and leaving the room.

In the room you have a stage where the moderator and the speakers are,

Everyone else is in the audience. In the front of the audience are the followers of the speakers.

Staring your own room means you can choose for the room to be Closed, Social or Open.

Events

Do you remember why events are so important to you? Do you remember how to create live events? Remember our dog trainer used events both on and off Clubhouse to build her brand and her business. She used the same specific dog icon for all her activities to reinforce her brand.

Remember when you first entered the Hallway, you had notifications and calendar tabs on the top of the page. All events that you might be interested in will be listed there. Add yours to this list. Click on the event tab and complete the information to set up your event. Are you moderating or are you the only speaker? Will our dog trainer bring in other famous dog trainers?

Your opportunities at this point are as broad as your imagination. Perhaps she would have an event with simultaneous rooms, one where she meets with users who want to start a pet care business and another with the famous dog trainers. Or perhaps there are three or four rooms with only one renowned trainer in each room. Users can pick the trainer that best meets their style, but every room is branded with Julie's Dog Training.

Clubs – what to remember

At the moment there is no easy way to search for a Club with your interests. Nor is it easy to start a Club. You have to search by user's profiles so be sure to get everyone in your room to follow you so you can get their profiles as well as following them.

Remember too that you have to earn your way into having your own Club(s). You earn this by showing you can effectively moderate rooms and be a speaker in other rooms. In this way you show your value to the Clubhouse staff and they reward you with a Club when you request it. This makes you the Founder of the Club.

Every Club has a Founder, members, followers, and non-Club followers. Each of these roles has different rights within the Club. Of course, the Founder can do everything. You write the description of the Club, the rules and set the icon. The Founder also decides if the room is private or public and who can stay in the room and who is deleted.

Members can create rooms in the Club that are private. They can see all the private rooms in the Club. Followers can only see the public rooms in the Club. They cannot create rooms or see private rooms. However, they are notified of all public rooms. Non-followers can participate in public Club rooms, but they are not notified about them.

Remember: You cannot just set up a Club from within the application. To set up a Club, you must request that the Clubhouse Team do so. This is a manual process and not something that the application can just do. This may change before the Clubhouse application goes public.

Is the Clubhouse Good for Business? Well, the simple answer is yes!

In fact, the rest of the book is spent giving you example after example of how and why this is true.

Building Your Brand

This is the topic you hear most about when discussing how to use Clubhouse to advance your business. Remember there is no better place online for a new entrepreneur to get his business financed and off the ground. There is no better place online for an experienced entrepreneur who wants to start a new line or an entirely new business. There is no better place online to discuss a career change or a complete change in your line of business.

The Clubhouse is not a place to make pitches and gain sales. It is however a place where the best will help the upcoming to succeed. On Clubhouse you learn what people think and what the current trends are in investments, startups, and creative ideas. Sure, there are pitfalls, but they are minor compared to the advantages of being on the Clubhouse.

I also mentioned a few other ways to monotonize your time on Clubhouse and these included:

- Be a paid moderator.
- Get paid to write other's bios and profiles.
- Be a paid speaker.
- Be a paid Networker – help others build their network.
- Be a paid Clubhouse coach.
- Be a paid Room Notetaker.

- Be a paid Connector.
- Be a paid Club Manager

Here is a final quick review of everything you need to do in the Clubhouse application in order to build your brand, market your products or services, gather followers and leads and increase your profits.

- Get invited and download the app.
- Spend time on your profile bio and picture. Tell users why they should follow you and what value you can add to their Clubhouse experience. Make sure your profile pictures are professional
- Use keywords to SEO (search engine optimization) your profile. Use powerful keywords. Remember the first three lines are the most important. Sell yourself to your followers. Stuff as many keywords into these three sentences as you can.
- Calls to Action in your profile. Like any good sales pitch your profile should have at least one call to action if not more. Remember, our dog trainer included not just her Twitter and Instagram, but her business URL as well. Encourage your followers to follow you off Clubhouse and to sites where they can purchase her services.
- Host rooms and events to share your expertise and promote yourself. Build Community through these activities with like-minded people. Establish your authority and credibility in your field in this way. Do not play games or try to be anyone but your authentic self. People do business with people they like. Share yourself selflessly. You can also start

private/closed rooms where once you have this credibility, you can charge a small group for your personal advice, knowledge, and mentoring.

- Start a Club so you can host multiple rooms simultaneously. You can schedule events for your Club in advance. The benefit of your Club is that all your followers might become members. At the very least all your followers will be notified of all your events. Remember starting you own Club lets you bring in outside speakers and host multiple rooms at the same time. Remember you need to host events before you get a Club.
- Host parties for all your new Clubhouse members. These are the people you bring into the Clubhouse either by offering them your invitation or wave them through when you see they downloaded the application. You can use a private room to welcome these newcomers and mentor them through their first few days on the site. You can also do this offsite, perhaps on YouTube or Zoom. By doing this off site you have the opportunity to pitch your products and services and direct them to your other sites. You can add to your authority and credibility by asking other users who are well known in your field to join your welcome party.
- As soon as you are comfortable get instant credibility and exposure by raising your hand and adding something of value to the discussion. This one act can bring you tens of followers.
- Use freebie to fill your room, build your brand and promote your business without making a single

sales pitch. Again, I take you back to our dog trainer who offered YouTube classes, raffled off training gift certificates or offered her book to all the people in the room who signed up as her follower. Do you remember the example of the speaker who discussed his business in an open room and collected enough leads from that room to meet his monthly sales quota in one day? You can accomplish these types of things yourself with these simple Calls to Action your freebies really are.

- Do not forget to ask others for feedback in your rooms and at your events. You want to learn what the trends are in your field and what your followers are thinking. Use DMs to your best advantage by talking off the application directly one to one with followers, potential customers and even investors.

The most important things to remember as you start out on this journey to build your brand awareness and market your business on Clubhouse are these few tasks.

- Collaborate with others/join or form teams
- Network with everyone you can. This is the catch phrase in business. Make it real.
- Establish your Authority and Credibility
- Build Community – One more time – people do business with people they like.
- Host a Viral Event – this is a key to your success.

Are you ready now? Are you anxious and excited to download the Clubhouse app. Maybe you already have your invitation all lined up. Follow the simple formulas in this book and soon you will have hundreds if not thousands of followers and potential clients.

Visit the Clubhouse every day and be present in the rooms you are in. Follow as many others as you can. They are likely to follow you as well. Host rooms, cohost rooms, host events and start Clubs as soon as you can. It is also a nice touch to invite your followers to other people's rooms and events that you are attending. As often as you can, find ways to mentor others both on and off the Clubhouse application. As I've said several times in the book, give of your knowledge, your expertise, and your passion. Give freely and graciously. What you give is certain to come back to you. Good luck and go clubbing!

To get access to **"Over the Shoulder"** training videos visit:

ClubhouseTraining.APP

If you're an Author, Speaker, Coach, or Entrepreneur looking for certainty, clarity, and a clear path to profit.

ACCELERATED POWER PIVOT SESSION

I would like to offer you a FREE **Accelerated Power Pivot Session**. During this session we will create a crystal clear vision, uncover hidden challenges that could be sabotaging your success and you will leave the session, re-energized and inspired.

Click the link below to schedule your FREE **Accelerated Power Pivot Session** with me personally.

I'm Ready, I'm Ready
Schedule My FREE Session

https://calendly.com/andybroadaway

Made in the USA
Monee, IL
05 November 2026

67387549R00085